BIBLICAL REVELATION
AND AFRICAN BELIEFS

BIBLICAL REVELATION AND AFRICAN BELIEFS

Edited by

KWESI A. DICKSON

and

PAUL ELLINGWORTH

LUTTERWORTH PRESS
UNITED SOCIETY FOR CHRISTIAN LITERATURE
LONDON

First published 1969
Second Impression 1970
Third Impression 1972

COPYRIGHT © 1969 ALL AFRICA CONFERENCE OF CHURCHES

Published with the help of a grant from
The Theological Education Fund

ISBN 0 7188 1652 8

Printed in Great Britain
by Page Bros. (Norwich) Ltd.

CONTENTS

ERRATA

p.135, line 3 from bottom for Buganda read **Baganda**
p.138, footnote 3 for Burundi read **Barundi**
p.159, footnote to read *Africa Theological Journal*
p.172, footnote 24 bottom line to read
Heilsgeschichte und Geschichte.
p.173, in the diagram the triangle indicating
"THIS AGE" should be extended so as to
terminate at the line marked "Parousia?"

FOREWORD

IN JANUARY, 1966, a consultation of African theologians was held at Immanuel College, Ibadan, Nigeria, under the auspices of the All Africa Conference of Churches (A.A.C.C.) and attended by participants, including two Roman Catholics, from a number of the universities of Africa, and representatives of the World Council of Churches and the A.A.C.C.

The consultation was an expression of a deep longing that the churches of Africa might have an opportunity of thinking together of the Christian faith which had come to them from the older churches of the West and through missionaries of a different cultural background who, in the nature of things, could not fully appreciate the reactions of their converts to their faith in the light of their own traditional beliefs and practices. Over a long period of growth the Church had taken root in Africa and there were indications that here and there individuals were beginning to examine the heritage of the Church to see how pertinently it related to African thought, ideas and life in a rapidly changing situation. The consultation was an opportunity for a number of qualified Africans to undertake the exercise together.

This book contains the principal papers presented at the consultation, some of which were revised in the light of discussion that followed each one. It has been an encouragement that a number of people who read about the consultation in the *A.A.C.C. Bulletin* asked for copies of the papers, and are looking forward to the report. The A.A.C.C. has already given permission for a few of the papers to be included in a German publication. It is hoped that the report will arouse discussion not only in the universities and theological colleges, but also in various church groups.

The consultation would not have been possible but for the generous grant of U.S. $10,000 by the Theological Education Fund (T.E.F.) and contributions by some universities in Africa

vii

and by some of the participants. Nor would the report have been produced but for the labour of love of the Editors—the Rev. Kwesi Dickson, of the University of Ghana, and the Rev. Paul Ellingworth (formerly of the Theological Faculty of Yaoundé, Cameroun). Together they prepared the English edition, and Mr. Ellingworth was responsible for the French edition. Their hard work, extending over a period of almost twenty months, was extra to their own normal heavy commitments.

On behalf of the A.A.C.C., which planned the consultation, I should like to express our indebtedness to all who supported it as participants, or continued its work, or contributed the funds which made it possible. The stimulus to the thinking of the churches by the Report will be their deepest satisfaction, and I hope that the fruit of that thinking will be shared with the A.A.C.C.

S. H. AMISSAH
General Secretary, A.A.C.C.

NEW NAMES have been given to certain geographical and administrative entities since these chapters were first written. Some designations are still in dispute, and no attempt at editorial revision has been made.

Cover drawing by Father E. Mveng; reproduced by permission of Father Mveng and Maison Mame, Tours.

INTRODUCTION

DURING THE All Africa Conference of Churches in 1963, it became quite clear to a number of us that the Church in Africa could only attain selfhood and be adequate for her mission when she possessed a first-hand knowledge of the Lord of the Church and was able to express that knowledge in clear accents made possible through her own original meditation and thinking.

It has become increasingly clear, and disturbingly so, that the Church has been speaking in Africa and to Africans in strange or partially understood tongues. We must be thankful to God that in spite of man's weaknesses and short-sightedness, the miracle of grace has been taking place all over Africa. Nevertheless, we realize that both the tools and the method of evangelism as employed in this continent are now calling very loudly for a careful overhauling.

Unfortunately, hitherto, evangelism in Africa has been based upon the false notion that Africa has nothing to offer as a cultural or spiritual basis for the Gospel. Hastily conducted anthropological and ethnological researches have given the impression that if the European educator or evangelist came to Africa, it must be to introduce something that was completely unrelated to the ways and wisdom of her peoples.

Leo Frobenius, in his book *The Voice of Africa*, tells us that before he visited Africa he had read a Berlin journal—a nineteenth-century document—which had this to say about Africa:

Before the introduction of a genuine faith and a higher standard of culture by the Arabs, the natives had no political organization, nor, strictly speaking, any religion . . . Therefore, in examining the pre-Muhammedan condition of the negro races, [we must] confine ourselves to the description of their crude fetishism, their brutal and often cannibalistic customs, their vulgar and repulsive idols. . . . None but the

9

most primitive instincts determine the lives and conduct of the negroes, who lacked every kind of ethical inspiration.[1]

Frobenius remarks that he noticed that the explorer Stanley had given to Africa the description of "dark" and "darkest", "a place governed by insensible fetish". Further, he quotes "a great light of the Church" as saying that "the 'niggers' have no souls and are burnt-out husks of men".

Edwin Smith tells of his conversation with an eminent biographer, Emil Ludwig. He had told Ludwig what the missionaries were doing in Africa—teaching the Africans about God. Ludwig was perplexed. Then he made his notorious remarks, "How can the untutored African conceive God? . . . How can this be? . . . Deity is a philosophical concept which savages are incapable of framing."[2]

Why this exhumation, at this time of the day, of things that should be dead and are better forgotten? But are they really dead? Do these preconceived notions belong only to the past? Some European theologians have for a while now been curious about other people's cultures; however, some of the most prolific authors see little or nothing that is of spiritual value in these cultures and religions. For example, it was Karl Barth's conviction that "all other religions are 'sin', the work of Godless man, or humanistic attempts at raising men to divine level".

Such attitudes arise, one imagines, in consequence of excessive zeal to defend the uniqueness of Christianity and to distinguish it from what in popular but ill-defined terms is described as "heathenism" or "paganism". But surely, if they are certain of their own faith and understand the facts of the Christian faith, should they not be aware that since Christ is *truly* unique, essential Christianity will always shine in its own light, especially through the lives of believers? God is able to defend His own cause, and that not by argument or debate, but by the communication of that life which is more abundant.

We must realize that excessive zeal to protect the Christian faith cannot but be a handicap to its propagation. It constitutes

[1] Vol. 1 (London, O.U.P., 1913), pp. xiii f.
[2] *African Ideas of God* (London, Edinburgh House Press, 1950: 2nd edn., 1961), p. 1.

a handicap because we begin by thinking that the effect of God's action depends upon our advocacy. The truth of the matter is, neither theology nor evangelism can be defined in terms of what *we* think that *we* want to teach and say to people. They are properly defined in terms of what God has done, what God is doing, and what God is saying to each people in their own native context. Theology and evangelism are not directions as to what *we* think that people should be or what we want them to be: they are declarations of God and His sovereign love and will to all peoples.

And that is why it is essential for theologians to distinguish carefully between "the action of God" and "the reaction of man". The former is constant and ever true with a cosmic significance; the latter may vary, depending as it does upon personal backgrounds, upbringing, moods and prejudices. We see here also the reason why the African theologian cannot afford the luxury of fixed ideas or of striving to conform himself to the category of a conservative or a liberal. Self-identification of this kind could lead to intellectual dishonesty and cramp orginality by closing the mind to truth. In C. S. Lewis's *Screwtape Letters* the apprentice tempter is instructed to exploit the darling tendency of his victim who "doesn't think of doctrines as primarily 'true' or 'false', but as 'academic' or 'practical', 'outworn' or 'contemporary', 'conventional' or 'ruthless'."[3] The African theologian must bear it constantly in mind that he is an apostle of Him who is the Truth, and that his main pursuit is that truth which makes free, not only from conventional sins and errors, but also from the subtle sins of prejudice and intolerance.

We must admit that the danger of idolatry (properly defined) and syncretism is always with us. But while we appreciate this danger, we have nevertheless to realize that we are only placing ourselves in a questionable position if in defence of truth we run away from truth. And half-truth is as much to be condemned as a denial of truth.

Let us be thankful to God that despite man's weaknesses, He has never left Himself without dedicated and discerning witnesses. In his first charge in 1867, Bishop Ajayi Crowther urged the Church "to know what has been done, in what way it has

---

[3] *Op. cit.*, (London, Bles, 1954), p. 11.

been done, to detect our errors and correct them, so as to be able to start with fresh vigour and earnestness in the strength of the Lord in this good work".[4] Later, in his instruction to his clergy, he said, "When we first introduce the Gospel to any people we should take advantage of any principles which they themselves admit. Thus, though the heathens in this part of Africa possess no written legends, yet wherever we turn our eyes, we find among them, in their animal sacrifices, a text which is the mainspring of Christian faith: 'Without shedding of blood there is no remission.' Therefore we may with propriety say: 'That which ye ignorantly practise, declare we unto you.' 'The blood of Jesus Christ the Son of God cleanseth from all sin.' "[5] Clearly, Bishop Crowther had realized the vital importance of communicating the Gospel to Africans in a language which they would understand.

Here we are led inevitably to the subject of "revelation". It is enough now to say that unless we get our theology right at this delicate point we shall continue to be, in our evangelistic efforts in Africa, little more than "babblers and chatterers, spendthrifts of our time". If we are true to the spirit of the Bible and of our faith, we must admit that God's self-disclosure is, in the first instance, to the whole world and that each race has grasped something of this primary revelation according to its native capability. To deny this, as some have been trying to do, is to approach theology with a cultural bias and be traitors to truth. As Professor H. H. Farmer says in his book, *Revelation and Religion,* "The idea of revelation is found, in more or less perspicuous form, in all religions; we could even say in all cultures." He maintains that the universal impulse to worship and the consequent practice of worship is a result of one central impulse—that of "one divine personal will seeking all the time to make itself known".[6] " . . . the one living and personal God" making Himself known, keeping a grip on men . . . this implicit sense of the one living God . . . when it became explicit, did so in a form conditioned by the general mental level and by the polytheistic system of ideas; it took the form of a belief in the one High God who is supreme over all and to whom all other

[4] Jesse Page, *The Black Bishop* (London, Simpkin, 1910), p. 277.
[5] *Ibid.*, p. 282.
[6] *Op. cit.* (London, Nisbet, 1954), p. 105 f.

supernatural powers are therefore subject . . . Belief in the High God was the primitive man's way of apprehending, and responding to, and expressing, the self-revealing pressure upon him of the one God."[7]

As I have pointed out elsewhere,[8] the question which we must face frankly is the one raised by C. H. Dodd in his book, *Gospel and Law*—". . . is the God of our redemption the same as the God of creation?" Even Kraemer was aware of a question with the same import: Is the God who spoke to Adam the same God who speaks through Jesus Christ?[9] To answer either question in the negative is to create an artificial divine vacuum between the creation and the moment of God's climactic revelation and thus land ourselves either in a subtle form of Marcionite dualism or in semi-deism.

There is no doubt that the urgent predicament of the Church in Africa today is that of the apparent foreignness of Christianity. And this, as we have pointed out, has resulted from the erroneous notion with which evangelism was bedevilled from the start. By a miscarriage of purpose the Church has succeeded in preaching to, and in teaching, Africans about a strange God whom they have somehow come to identify as the God of the white man. But what has happened to the God as known to their forbears—the God who is the foundation of their traditional beliefs? He remains still with them. And so we have left them with two Gods in their hands and thus made of them peoples of ambivalent spiritual lives. This impedes the progress of evangelism; it also results in a very dangerous kind of polytheism. Indeed, African nationalism is already calling into being a political God of Africa in contradistinction to the God of the Europeans whom a prominent politician once described as a God of oppression, a God of greed and injustice.

Of course, the Church only cuts the ground from under her own feet if, by a deliberate act, or through carelessness in her theology, she preaches a God who is the possession of any particular section of the human race. This would be a God who is "too small" and therefore cannot be the God and Father of our Lord Jesus Christ.

[7] H. H. Farmer, *ibid.*, p. 109.
[8] E. Bolaji Idowu, *Towards An Indigenous Church* (London, O.U.P., 1965), p. 25.
[9] *Religion and the Christian Faith* (London, Lutterworth, 1956), ch. 14.

One of the major assignments before those who seek to communicate and inculcate the Gospel in Africa is that of understanding Africa and appreciating the fact that they must learn to address Africans as Africans. As Ernst Benz has warned, "One of the first difficulties to confront even an experienced enquirer into foreign religions is in fact that he more or less unconsciously takes his own point of view as normative for religions in general. It is difficult to avoid this pitfall . . . The mental habits of Western Christians and their philosophical presuppositions are carried into their field of study . . . and so this makes it difficult for them to understand the set-up in another culture or tradition".[10] This applies also to those Africans whose outlook has become "Westernized".

We must lay to heart also the warning of the Reverend Placide Tempels: "Any one who wishes to study primitive people . . . must give up all idea of attaining valid scientific conclusions so long as he has not been able to understand their metaphysic. To declare on *a priori* grounds that primitive peoples have no ideas on the nature of beings, that they have no ontology and that they are completely lacking in logic, is simply to turn one's back on reality. Every day we are able to note that primitive peoples are by no means children who are just afflicted with a bizarre imagination. It is as Men that we have learned to know them in their home."[11] Tempels goes on to write, ". . . a better understanding of the realm of Bantu thought is just as indispensable for all who are called upon to live among native people. It therefore concerns . . . all who wish to civilize, educate and raise the Bantu. But, if it concerns all colonisers with good will, it concerns most particularly missionaries.[12]

"If one has not penetrated into the depths of the Bantu personality as such, if one does not know on what basis they act, it is not possible to understand the Bantu. One is entering into no spiritual contact with them. One cannot make oneself intelligible to them, especially in dealing with the great spiritual realities. On the contrary, one runs the risk, while believing that one is civilizing the individual, of in fact corrupting him—work-

---

[10] "Obstacles to Understanding other Religions", in *Relations Among Religions Today* (Leiden, Brill, 1963), p. 101.

[11] *Bantu Philosophy* (Paris, Présence Africaine, 1959), p. 16.

[12] *Ibid.*, p. 17.

ing to increase the numbers of the deracinated and to become the architect of revolts."[13]

The task of knowing Africa is not an easy one, however. There are several factors which may create handicaps. The size of Africa is a formidable problem to honest enquirers. So also are her complex cultures and almost innumerable languages and myriads of dialects. In certain parts of Africa the aboriginal peoples have been wiped out, and therefore also the racial memory, in consequence of European settlements. There are areas where, for various reasons, the aboriginal peoples had been forced to be on the move over a long period, with the result that they have become scattered and settled among other peoples; in such a case their identities have become either confused or lost, and the racial memory has suffered the same fate. The policy of direct and indirect colonial indoctrination as well as that of assimilation have left their effects for better or for worse on Africa. All over Africa people have been led to the stage of despising their own native traditions and cultures and of regarding foreign ideas and cultures as the only way to human dignity. There are those areas where people find a curious compensation under gross oppression and exploitation in striving to forget their antecedents and identifying themselves with the cultures of their oppressors. We have also to reckon with the inevitable fact of death. The old, knowledgeable repositories of African oral traditions have either died, or are dying out, and so are no longer available for interview or consultation: a great loss has taken place in this area. And there are the influences of other religions and cultures: as generation after generation of Africans embrace a new religion or culture, they tend to abandon and forget the traditions of their own indigenous beliefs, ways and wisdom. This is so especially where they have been effectively convinced that their antecedents are all of the devil.

Nevertheless, we have enough still for the purpose of research. Only we have to be quick. With careful planning and coordination, regular consultations and conversations, we shall eventually succeed in bringing out something truly useful and illuminating.

It is only when the Church in Africa has undertaken to ad-

[13] *Ibid.*, pp. 16 ff.

dress herself to the task of evangelism with a view to making it relevantly purposeful that she can be alive to her responsibility and meet the challenges of a situation which is daily becoming more and more alarmingly complex.

The main theme before us in this symposium is "Biblical Revelation and African Beliefs". Thus, we set ourselves the task of finding an answer to the delicate question of whether there is any correlation between the Biblical concept of God and the African concept of God, between what God has done and is doing according to Biblical record and teaching and what God has done and is doing in Africa according to African traditional beliefs. We seek to find Biblical answers to the spiritual yearnings of the hearts of Africans, what Christianity offers as the satisfaction to the urge in them towards true personal maturity and selfhood, and a corporate personality. We seek, in effect, to discover in what way the Christian faith could best be presented, interpreted, and inculcated in Africa so that Africans will hear God in Jesus Christ addressing Himself immediately to them in their own native situation and particular circumstances.

The consultation of African theologians held at Ibadan in 1965, of which the present symposium is the result, summed up its work in the following statement:

> We believe that the God and Father of our Lord Jesus Christ, Creator of heaven and earth, Lord of history, has been dealing with mankind at all times and in all parts of the world. It is with this conviction that we study the rich heritage of our African peoples, and we have evidence that they know of Him and worship Him.
>
> We recognise the radical quality of God's self-revelation in Jesus Christ; and yet it is because of this revelation we can discern what is truly of God in our pre-Christian heritage: this knowledge of God is not totally discontinuous with our people's previous traditional knowledge of Him.

I

GOD

He raised his grey old head. "It is written in the Fourth
Surah, 'Men's souls are naturally inclined to covetousness,
but if ye be kind towards women and fear to wrong them,
God is well acquainted with what ye do.' "
. . . The other women looked at her curiously. "I saw you
sitting with the headman, chatting away," said one . . .
". . . What did he talk about?"
Jean thought for a minute. "This and that . . . He talked
about God a little."
The women started at her, "You mean, his own God?
Not the real God?"
"He didn't differentiate," Jean said. "Just God."[1]

"He didn't differentiate," Jean said. "Just God." Jean's
statement is balancing on a razor's edge. What exactly is in her
mind? The position of "the women" is clear. "The real God"
is their own God; the headman's God is not the real God!
And precisely this is where we come in at this moment: to
decide first of all whether any people—of whatever creed or
colour or race—have any right to claim God as *their own* in
such a possessive way like "the women"; whether any people
have a right to speak of "our God" and "their God"; whether
a God who could be fitted into the category of the sole possession
of any people or race could in any way be the same God whom
Jesus Christ came to reveal and whom essential Christian faith
holds as "The Lord . . . the everlasting God, the Creator of
the ends of the earth."
This is a vital point, and we cannot really proceed to discuss God or anything relating to our faith until we have

[1] Nevil Shute, *A Town Like Alice* (London, Pan Books edn., 1961), p. 60.

settled it. For here we strike the question of the knowledge of God, whether every race has something of this knowledge, however primary, or whether any peoples could be said to have been completely excluded from it.

Andrew Lang in *The Making of Religion* has claimed that "many savage tribes are as monotheistic as many Christians".[2] Father Schmidt of Vienna, who actually researched into the beliefs of the "pigmies" of the Congo, claims in *The Origin and Growth of Religion* that the belief in, and worship of, one Supreme Deity is universal among all really primitive peoples; that the "High God" is found everywhere among them sufficiently prominently to make his position indubitable; that he is not a late development or traceable to missionary influences. He holds that the belief encircles the whole earth like a girdle and that it "is an essential property of whatever ancient human culture existed in the very earliest time . . . before the individual groups had separated from one another". The Supreme Being of the primitive culture is a genuinely monotheistic Deity, described as Father, Creator, eternal, completely beneficent, ethically holy, and creatively omnipotent.

The reaction of European scholars to the conclusions of Father Schmidt is typical. A. C. Bouquet, the Cambridge specialist in Comparative Religion, has his doubts and would rather think that primitive peoples could never develop such ideas apart from "contact with some group of monotheists". In any case, he concluded, Father Schmidt's evidence was not proved![3]

Despite the accumulation of evidence from the work of Andrew Lang, Söderblom, and Father Schmidt and others, emotional resentment and deliberate refusal to accept facts on the part of some European scholars have resulted in the erroneous theory of "the high gods of primitive peoples". As I have maintained in *God in Nigerian Belief*,[4] if ever there is a god who is a figment of man's imagination, it is this "high god"; for he is only "an academic invention, an intellectual marionette whose behaviour depends upon the mental partiality of its

[2] Quoted by John Oman in *The Natural and The Supernatural* (Cambridge, 1931), p. 385.
[3] See A. C. Bouquet, *Man and Deity* (Heffer, Cambridge, 1933), p. 101 f.
[4] (Lagos, Federal Ministry of Information, 1963), p. 9.

creators. Therefore, he could be made to withdraw from the life and thought of the people, could be lent features and a face, could be made to be just everything that would preclude the slightest suspicion of a revelation from the Living God." These scholars have furnished us with an unnecessary, artificial pluralism. For they do not hesitate to concede to each nation, people, or "tribe," its own "high god", with the result that the whole place is overrun with "high gods" of various brands. P. A. Talbot, in his book *The Peoples of Southern Nigeria*, writes, "In practically every tribe, there is a Supreme God. . . . "[5] This "primitive high god" is a product of ignorance and prejudice. There are too many stay-at-home investigators on the job, while those who go out into the field often find it difficult to leave behind at home their own preconceived notions.

For the Christian theologian who is committed to the facts of "In the beginning God . . .", and "The earth is the Lord's and the fulness thereof, the world and those who dwell therein", Father Schmidt's assertion that the belief in God "encircles the whole earth like a girdle", and "is an essential property of whatever ancient human culture existed in the very earliest times" should not appear strange. For the Creator Spirit who like a mother-bird sat upon the primordial chaos and out of that chaos of non-existence brought forth order, cohesion, meaning and life has certainly left the mark of His creative activity upon the created order. This is the primary stage of revelation—something through which the Creator is revealed. Then He created man in His own image—a rational being, intelligent will, someone address-able and therefore responsible (= response-able): someone to whom God could communicate His revelation through his appreciation of the created order and with whose spirit the Divine Spirit could have immediate communication. We can deny this primary revelation only when we rob the created order of its revelatory quality and relieve man of his inherent capability to receive divine communication. In the words of Eliade, "For religious man, the world always presents a supernatural valence, that is, it reveals a modality of the sacred. Every cosmic fragment is transparent; its own mode of existence *shows* a particular struc-

[5] Vol. II (London, O.U.P., 1926), p. 15.

ture of being, and hence of the sacred."[6] "God's essence", says Kegley in interpreting Brunner, "is the will to self-communication."[7] And DeWolf says, "A revelation must be made to a rational being", ". . . it is God Who is directly made known rather than ideas about Him."[8] All this is summed up in St. Paul's words in Romans 1: 20—"Ever since the creation of the world his invisible nature, namely, his eternal power and deity has been clearly perceived in the things that have been made." The same fact is emphasized by John Baillie in his book *Our Knowledge of God*: he quotes Canon Lilley as saying, "God may create a universe *ex nihilo*, but He cannot reveal Himself *ad nihilum*. . . . We may say that apart from actual communion with God there is no worthy and complete human personality. But we may also say that apart from some incipient degree of personality there would be nothing for God to communicate with."[9] Further, Baillie observes that not one of us has been left quite alone by God, that we have been brought out from the beginning, that from the beginning we have possessed more light than we have used. "Man has spirit", writes Brunner, "only in that he is addressed by God. . . . Therefore the human self is nothing which exists in its own right, no property of man, but a relation to a divine Thou."[10]

We maintain, therefore, that God cannot be confined in any way. His realm is the whole universe. All peoples are His concern. And He has revealed Himself primarily to them all, each race apprehending the revelation according to its native capability. ". . . the growth of religion would have been impossible if there had not been at least one fact—the personality of God—which it not merely started from, but to which it constantly returns, and in which, properly understood, it finds its constant touchstone of truth".[11]

The next point for us to examine is whether any people or

[6] Mircea Eliade, *The Sacred and the Profane* (New York, Harper Torchbooks, 1961), p. 138.
[7] Charles W. Kegley, *The Theology of Emil Brunner* (New York, Macmillan, 1962), p. 183.
[8] L. Harold DeWolf, *A Theology of the Living Church* (New York, Harper, 1960), pp. 32 and 36.
[9] *Our Knowledge of God* (London, O.U.P., 1941), p. 26.
[10] *Ibid.*, pp. 3 ff., 42.
[11] F. B. Jevon, "Anthropomorphism", in *Encyclopedia of Religion and Ethics*, Vol. 1. (Edinburgh, Clark, 1908), p. 576.

creed can claim to possess a *clear* knowledge of God in an absolute sense. This point is very important for us; it is not infrequently that we hear it glibly stated that Africans have no clear concept of God. This arises largely from the unexamined premise that because Europeans have written systematic statements about God, therefore they have a clear concept of God. Is there not a world of difference between an actual, saving knowledge of God and an academic "knowledge" of Him—a thing reached and written down through a process of ratiocination, which might make little or no difference to the life either of the writer or the reader? We tend to forget also that the prophetic insight with regard to the nature of God is always far in advance of the general concept of Him held by the generality of the people. Moreover, the emphasis of the Bible is that God reveals Himself . . . God cannot be fully known. "Truly, thou art a God who hidest thyself, O God of Israel, the Saviour" (Isaiah 45: 15); "Can you find out the deep things of God? Can you find out the limit of the Almighty?" (Job 11:7). These are statements which are expressive of man's baffling plight in his spiritual attempt to solve the riddle with which he is confronted by God's being and nature.

When Western philosophy and theology apply the word "Person" to God, they are only using a descriptive, figurative term. We shall find that much as we may try to avoid it, the word will have no meaning for us unless God is in a way anthropomorphically conceived. And when we intelligently set the teaching that God is Person side by side with the concept that "God is Spirit", we see immediately how much of a riddle we have on our hands.

Recent publications in Europe and America have come to indicate how much confusion there is in the minds even of the enlightened Westerners about God. If we take for example some of the writings of Dietrich Bonhoeffer, the writings of Paul Tillich, and *Honest To God* of Dr. J. A. T. Robinson, we shall see at least two facts clearly emerging: the fact that the masses of Westerners appear to be losing their sense of God, and Western theology is in conflict because it has become too theoretical: God according to it has become largely an intellectual concept.

According to H. Wheeler Robinson in *The Christian Experience of the Holy Spirit,* Sadhu Sundar Singh had a vision, and in relating this vision he said, "When I entered heaven for the first time I looked all round me and then I asked: 'Where is God?' and they answered and said to me: 'God is seen here as little as on earth, for God is infinite. But Christ is here, He is the image of the Invisible God, and only in Him can anyone see God, either here or upon earth.' "[12]

It is because of the very weakness of our perception that God in His infinite love and mercy caused the Word to become flesh and pitch His tent among us. Even then, God in Jesus is known only to as many as will receive Him—those who spiritually discern and accept that in Him is God (John 1: 14, 9–13).

All this is to warn us that nowhere is the concept of God clear in an absolute sense. In fact, more likely than not, it is clearer to those who grasp the fact of God intuitively and know Him to be the very basis of their existence and the ultimate motive of their lives than it is to those who are able to read about Him in books for pleasure, to satisfy curiosity, or as an intellectual exercise, and no more. We know this in consequence of our bafflement when we are confronted with certain basic questions about the nature of God which we have no spiritual resources to face, or whenever we are faced with acute social or moral problems which by their nature raise questions with regard to the reality of God and the government or the very purpose of the universe. Isaiah's and Job's exclamations as quoted above, and Luther's famous phrase, *Deus absconditus et revelatus,* are not academic; they are expressions by worshipping but baffled human souls. *Deus absconditus et revelatus* is always urging Himself upon us anywhere and everywhere; but quite often we see the *absconditus* rather than, or more than, the *revelatus* aspect, because of our finitude. Therefore, when the theologian takes a look at other people's religion, before he asserts glibly that there is no concept of God, let him look within his own system, or, better still, within himself. If he is honest and he is not just someone setting one religion against another in competition, he will at least concede that here is a mystery with which people are grappling according to their own native capabilities. He will avoid rushing to facile conclusions.

[12] (London, Nisbet, 1944), p. 67.

I have no time and space to quote and criticise more of the things which have been said about belief in God according to African traditional religion. Suffice it here to quote Herskovits: "The assertion of the existence of the belief among West Africans that the Creator, having made the world, left it to its own devices and the pleasure of inferior gods, found so often in literature must be viewed as defining the traditional European approach to African religions."[13]

Now, where do we go from here? Should the theologian, because of the basic difficulty that we have outlined above, pray in the language of Ronald Knox's limerick:

O God, forasmuch as without Thee
We are not enabled to doubt Thee,
    Help us all by Thy grace
    To convince the whole race
It knows nothing whatever about Thee.[14]

We cannot do this, because the heart of the prayer is false. We only need to achieve a clear perspective: to know that God is God and that we are only creatures. Our major difficulty begins and we are confused in our ideas only when we forget this and seek to prescribe for God the bounds of the operation of His Spirit. Our calling is to accept that which God Himself gives and commissions, and transmit this to the world. That means that a theologian who thinks that he is an intellectualist is only wasting his time. A theologian who is worthy of the name is first and foremost a man of prayer, waiting upon God for a message, God's own message.

With regard to Africa, I have outlined briefly in the "Introduction" those things which constitute our difficulty in the acquisition of first-hand knowledge of Africa and her peoples. I have also indicated what I consider to be a fruitful line of approach. There is no doubt that from the honest research that has been done and that is being done, we have enough material to begin with. And here is a challenge: each of us must get to know his own people thoroughly, and approach

[13] M. J. Hershovits, *Dahomey* (New York, Augustin, 1938), Vol. I, p. 289.
[14] From *The Complete Limerick Book*, ed. Langford Reed (London, Jarrolds, 1925). Reprinted in R. A. Knox: *In Three Tongues*, ed. L. E. Eyres (London, Chapman & Hall, 1959), p. 123.

their belief reverently and sympathetically, because we possess that which is the key to their soul—the language.

We begin by looking at the African concept of God first because this is the key to all that we seek to achieve at, and as a result of, this Consultation. In the words of Tillich, "a religious statement, where God is not the *prius* of everything, you never can reach Him. . . . If you don't start with Him, you never can reach Him."[15]

In *Nupe Religion*, S. F. Nadel says, "The most basic concept of Nupe theology, that of the supreme being, is also the widest. In a sense it stands for the whole realm of religion . . .[16] Let us begin here and we shall find the following true with regard to the concept of God in Africa.

(a) *God is real to Africans*

We can speak of a many-sided concept of God in Africa. This is in consequence of linguistic and cultural variations by which it has been affected. It is not infrequently that foreign investigators over-emphasize or exaggerate these elements of variation and therefore fail to see the basic unity, concluding, as they have sometimes done, that it is all amorphous.

God is real to Africans and that is why Africans call Him by names which are descriptive both of His nature and of His attributes. A study of these names will afford us a very deep insight into the African concept of God. Unfortunately, we cannot be quite certain about the derivations or history of several of the principal names in consequence of their age, but especially because we have no written literature about the ancient past of Africa to guide us. *African Ideas of God*, edited by Edwin Smith and recently revised by E. Geoffrey Parrinder, has placed this difficulty before us in clear terms. Edwin Smith warns that "Etymological methods are not invariably helpful and indeed may easily lead astray. It is impossible to recover the primary meanings of some of the old African names for the Supreme Being. . . . This philological region is the happy hunting ground of fantastic etymologists. Certain writers seem to be supremely ambitious to find origins outside Africa

---

[15] Mimeographed lectures on "A History of Christian Thought" (1953), ed. C. E. Braaten (London, S.C.M. Press, 1968).
[16] *Nupe Religion* (London, Routledge & Kegan Paul, 1954), p. 10.

for African ideas . . . and they make great play with verbal similarities."[17] Nevertheless, the words of R. S. Rattray, *Ashanti*,[18] J. B. Danquah, *The Akan Doctrine of God*,[19] and the present writer's *Olodumare: God In Yoruba Belief*,[20] to quote a few well-known examples, have, besides underlining the fact that it is necessary to be careful, showed us how much may be derived and gained from the study of the names through a thorough knowledge of the people and language as well as through patient and careful research. Besides the names, we have the clearly expressed attributes of God according to African beliefs. In fact, it is through these that we discover the wealth of meaning in the African conception of Him. It may not be possible in every case to arrive at the primary meaning of a principal name of the Supreme Being, but the praise-names, titles or epithets always throw much light upon the people's ideas.

In *Olodumare*, I have tried to analyse some of the Yoruba names for God. I wish here to draw attention to one in particular. It is *Orişe*. This is an ancient name of God which is not universally employed today among the Yoruba, though it is commonly used among the Owo people (of Yorubaland) and among the Itsekiri and Western Ijaw. This name by derivation falls into two parts—*ori* and *se*. *Ori* is the essence of being and in the name of God it means "the very Source of Being" or "Source-Being". *Se* is a verb meaning "to originate". Thus the whole name means "the Source-Being which gives origin to all beings" or "the Source of all beings". This name occurs in various forms in several parts of Nigeria and in Dahomey. Among the Igbo we have a name which carries a similar or somewhat identical meaning and connotation. That is *Chukwu*. This also falls into two parts—*Chi* and *Ukwu*. Chi is a very pregnant word. It carries the connotation of an overflowing fullness, the Main-Source or Main-Essence of Being. *Ukwu* means great, immense; it has also the connotation of a bundle or "that which contains". *Chi-ukwu* thus means "the Immense, Overflowing Source of Being".

Both *ori* and *chi* are also the names of the essence of human

---

[17] *African Ideas of God* (London, Edinburgh House Press, 1961), p. 3; 2nd ed., London, Frank Cass & Co., 1968.

[18] (London, O.U.P., 1955.)

[19] (London, Lutterworth Press, 1944.)

[20] E. Bolaji Idowu, *Olodumare, God In Yoruba Belief* (London, Longmans, 1962).

personality, that which makes a person a person, that apart from which a person is not a living being, that upon which personal destiny depends. It is in connection with personal destiny that *ori* or *chi* becomes a semi-split entity which assumes the role of man's guardian-angel.

Let us look in this connection also at the name *ɔdomankoma*—one of the Akan names of God. Here centres the Akan conception of God as Creator. The main point here is that He is the Creator, creating out of his own overflowing fullness. In Danquah's words, the name means "He who is uninterruptedly, infinitely and exclusively full of the manifold, namely, the interminable, eternally, infinitely, universally filled entity".[21]

With the idea expressed in *Oriṣe*, *Chukwu*, and *Ɔdomankoma*, I would connect the words of Psalm 104.29, 30—"Thou takest away their breath, they die. . . . Thou sendest thy spirit, they are created", and of Acts 17:28—"In him we live and move and have our being. . . . For we are indeed his off-spring."

And it is precisely in consequence of this belief that it is categorically stated by Africans that even though God may commission a divinity to mould man's physical parts, it belongs to Him and Him alone to put the essence of being in man. God "breathed into his nostrils the breath of life; and man became a living being" (Genesis 2:7); this is asserted unmistakably, though in various ways, in Africa.

I should like to mention in concluding this section that the Akan principal name of God, *Onyame* or *'Nyame*, which is very difficult or almost impossible now to translate, would appear to be related to the God-name *Nyambe* which occurs in several parts of Africa (Nigeria, Cameroon, Central Africa, etc.) in various forms, such as *Yambe*, *Ndyambi*, etc. The possibility of there being a basic linguistic, racial and cultural foundation underlying these names is well worth investigating.

(b) *God is unique*

We have this conception clearly stated according to the beliefs of several African peoples. One may make bold to say that the conception is universal throughout Africa. Both the

[21] *Op. cit.*, 1st. edn., p. 61 ff.

Yoruba and the Edo (Nigeria) express in several ways the fact
that He is incomparable. There are myths to this effect. The
Tiv (Nigeria) believe that He surpasses all. This is why graven
images or paintings of God are non-existent, or almost non-
existent, because there is nothing to compare to Him. J. B.
Danquah translates the name *Onyankopon* (Akan) as "The
Only Great Shining One", or "He who alone is of the Greatest
Brightness".[22]

His uniqueness includes also the conception of His transcendence. J. B. Danquah gives the name *Onyame* (Akan) the meaning of "a shining living being elevated above, beyond the ordinary reach of man, but manifest to them through His light
which is visible even to a child".[23] The sense of His uniqueness
and transcendence as expressed in African thought and emphasized in their practices is partly the reason why God as
conceived by Africans is being wrongly described by European
investigators as a "withdrawn God".

(c) *The Universe is under unitary control—God's control*

There is a saying of the Nupe (Nigeria), "Soko is in front,
He is in the back".[24] This sums up what the people think
about God and the universe.

The conception of God as the Creator is expressed in various
ways. Often we are told that He commissions some works of
creation through a certain divinity. But creation originated
from Him. The Igbo (Nigeria) God-name *Chineke* (*chi-na-eke*)
means *Chi*-who-creates. We have referred to the Akan name
Odomankoma. The Nupe have a song, "A being which Soko
did not create, neither did the world create it".[25] They believe
that He is especially responsible for the ultimate issues of life
and death.

God is often described as King and Supreme. The Yoruba
(Nigeria) call Him *Oba Orun*—King Who is in heaven. The
Igbo call Him *Eze elu* or *Eze di n'elu*—King of heaven or King
Who is in heaven. There is a saying of the Mende (Sierra
Leone) that "God is the Chief";[26] and the Akan refer to God as

---

[22] *Op. cit.*, p. 45. [23] *Op. cit.*, pp. 38 f.
[24] S. F. Nadel, *op. cit.*, p. 11. [25] *Ibid.*, p. 12.
[26] K. L. Little, *The Mende of Sierra Leone* (London, Routledge and Kegan Paul,
1951), p. 218.

"the great God of the Sky who, of all the earth, is the King and Elder".[27] With regard to authority, the Nupe say that He is the only One and none other exists and so they call Him *Tsoci*—"the Owner of us", i.e. "our Lord".[28] There is a Yoruba saying to the effect that the divinities render Him regular tribute because He is the Head.[29] Every year, pilgrimages are made to the Temple of Nana Buluku at Doumé (Dahomey) and certain portions of offerings to Mawu-Lisa (arch-divinity) made anywhere in the land must be sent to this temple. It is believed that the divinities go there regularly to render accounts of their doings.

As king He is believed to be omnipotent. The Tiv believe that He surrounds the whole world, with moon, sun and stars under His control; and the Nupe say that "should you do anything that is beautiful, Soko has caused it to be beautiful; should you do anything evil, Soko has caused it to be evil".[30] Here we may compare Isaiah 45: 7—"I form light and create darkness, I make weal and create woe, I am the Lord, who do all these things."

As king He is the Judge. According to the Yoruba, there is a retributive principle which He has set in operation and in consequence of which sinners will not go unpunished.[31] The Igbo believe that He dispenses reward and punishment according to man's deserts, as may be seen in daily occurrences of life. The conception of the judgment of God is so strong that "the Wrath of God" has been conceptualized in a certain divinity. This is the solar and thunder divinity. This divinity has a very suggestive name among the Nupe. He is called *Sokogba* (*Soko egba*)—"God's axe". And it is illuminating that it is *Onyame* Himself who has custody of this axe according to Akan belief. There is a neolithic celt called '*Nyame Akuma* (God's axe) which is always inside His shrine.

(d) *God is universal*

The most suggestive name in this regard among Nigerians is the Edo name for God. This is *Osanobwa*. The first part *Osa* we have met before: it is a contraction of *Orişę*. The whole name

---

[27] R. S. Rattray, *op. cit.*, pp. 142, 144.
[28] S. F. Nadel, *op. cit.*, p. 11.   [29] E. Bolaji Idowu, *op. cit.*, p. 55.
[30] S. F. Nadel, *op. cit.*, p. 12.   [31] E. Bolaji Idowu, *op. cit.*, p. 146.

means "God Who carries or sustains the Universe". He is the Creator Who brought all things into being. It will be very illuminating to study the myths of all the places in Africa which are regarded as the centre of the earth, the place where creation began and from which the children of the great father dispersed all over the earth. We have a few such places in Nigeria and there is at least a suggestion that there is one in the land of the Akan. Ile-Ifẹ is the sacred city of the Yoruba, and it is believed that here the work of the creation of the earth began and that from here all the people of the earth originated and dispersed.[32] The force of this tradition is that the whole earth belongs to God, that one God created all, and that He "belongs" to all mankind.

From the above we should appreciate that there is a wealth of material with regard to the concept of God in Africa. What is even more important, we should realize that Africans have their own distinctive concepts of God and that God according to African traditional belief is not "a loan-God from the missionaries".

[32] E. Bolaji Idowu, op. cit., p. 11 ff.

2

GOD, SPIRITS AND THE SPIRIT WORLD

(With special reference to the Igbo-speaking[1] people of Southern Nigeria)

As PROFESSOR IDOWU has written in his introduction: "It has become increasingly clear, and disturbingly so, that the Church has been speaking in Africa and to Africans in strange or partially understood tongues. . . . We realize that both the tools and the method of evangelism as employed in this continent are now calling very loudly for a careful overhauling."[2]

There is, indeed, a universal outcry today, perhaps more than ever before, for this imperative and urgent overhauling of our method of evangelization. Africa, as a whole, is rapidly becoming more and more aware of her God-given and inalienable dignity and fundamental rights, and of the necessity of restoring the dignity of man. Today, the African no longer apologises for his existence on the face of the earth or for the pigment of his skin. Rather, he gladly sees himself as a piece of mosaic which the Divine Artist, in His eternal design, fashioned

---

[1] There are about nine million Igbo-speaking people, spread in various provinces of Southern Nigeria. Until recently, many writers, including Igbo writers themselves, have kept to the version "Ibo", which avoids the double consonant "gb" whose proper pronunciation is difficult for non-Igbo speakers of the language, especially the expatriates. This version, a corruption of the original word, "Igbo", seems to have been introduced by the early Europeans as an easy way out of the difficult pronunciation. Today, however, both the Government of Eastern Nigeria and many modern writers have replaced the Westernized form with the original: cp. C. O. Okoreaffia, "Multi-lingualism in the New Africa", International Press, Aba, 1962, passim: F. C. Ogbalu, *Omenala Igbo* (The Book of Igbo Custom), Onitsha, University Publishing Company, 1965, passim.

[2] See above, page 9; cp. also M. Marioghae and J. Ferguson, *Nigeria under the Cross* (London, Highway Press, 1965), pp. 71 ff.

to radiate in his own ways and environment as African in His infinite wisdom and splendour.

The wonderful and admirable diversity which we find in languages, colour and, in short, in all aspects of culture all over the world, goes to emphasize the ingenuity of the Maker of this noble piece of work which we call man. For, in spite of these diversities, human nature remains essentially the same throughout the world and throughout the ages and is destined to fulfilment in the one God of all the earth.

In exercising her divine mission of teaching all nations,[3] the Church must preach to the people in the language they will understand: the Church must try to adapt herself to different environments. She has no choice. She must adapt herself or face the inevitable consequences.

In this paper I shall try to outline, in the first part, the principles which should serve as a guide to those who are trying to disseminate the Faith. In the second part I shall briefly state what Africans believe about God, spirits and the spirit world. Finally, in the third part, an attempt will be made to suggest ways in which the principles in question might be applied in given situations.

I. THE PRINCIPLES OF ADAPTATION

Today, there is such universal awareness of the need for adapting the Gospel message to the different peoples that one gets the impression that adaptation is one of the discoveries of this scientific age of the twentieth century. The truth is that we are simply becoming more and more aware of, and trying to put into practice, the law of the apostolate which the Divine Teacher and Pastor of souls, who came not to destroy the law or the prophets but to fulfil,[4] promulgated and practised by His incarnation and by making Himself all things to all men even to the point of annihilating Himself;[5] which law the Apostles themselves applied and which has been handed down to us without interruption.

Christ did not send the Apostles to preach until He had im-

---

[3] Matt. 28:19, 20.   [4] Matt. 5:17.
[5] Cp. C. Rebesher, *Convert Making*, New York, Bruce, 1937, p. 140: "Christ's pedagogic method remains the classic pattern of the psychological approach even in this day of advanced method in the art of teaching."

parted to them the gift of tongues;[6] the Apostles themselves faithfully followed the example of their Divine Master. St. Paul tells us that he made himself all things to all men in order to gain all.[7]

Spreading of Christ The history of the Church, from the beginning to the present day, furnishes us with copious examples of adaptation. We know that in the early days of the Church common vessels were used, having been turned from profane to sacred use, and there were chalices of gold, silver, bones, ivory and, in poorer churches, of wood. St. Augustine, the Apostle of England, following the instruction received from St. Gregory the Great, consecrated pagan temples and turned them into places of worship after having destroyed the idols. He also made use of the vessels which he found there.[8]

Tertullian asserts that though human nature is tainted with original sin, owing to Adam's fall, yet it has in itself something that is naturally Christian.[9] It all means that the human soul, whether it belongs to the black or white race, and wherever it is found, naturally aspires after goodness in the environment in which it is found. St. Basil observes that "when we become accustomed to looking at the reflection of the sun in the water we shall turn to gaze upon the sun itself. . . . Certainly, the essential function of a tree is to produce fruit in season; still the foliage that its branches also bear, serves to adorn it. In the same way, the primary fruit of the soul is truth itself; but the garb of natural culture is a welcome addition just as leaves provide shade for the fruit and add to its beauty. Thus Moses, a man of the greatest renown for his wisdom, is said to have come to the contemplation of Him who is, only after being trained in Egyptian lore. So later, the wise Daniel is said to have been first schooled in Babylon in the wisdom of the Chaldeans, and only then to have come to know Divine Revelation."[10]

As far back as 1659 the Sacred Congregation for the Propagation of the Faith issued a very strongly worded instruction to

---

[6] Acts 2:4. [7] I Cor. 9:22.

[8] Cp. C. Costantini, "La Suppelletile Ecclesiastica nei paesi di missione", in *Il Pensiero Missionario* 4 (1934), 405.

[9] Cp. Tertullian, *Apologeticum*, cap. XVII.

[10] St. Basil, "Ad Adolescentes", 2, Migne, *Patrologia Series Graeca*, Paris, XXXI, 567A.

the Apostolic Vicars for the Foreign Missions working in China. This instruction, though directed primarily to missionaries then working in China, was meant to be of universal application. The instruction reads: "Do not show any zeal, and do not for any motive try to persuade those peoples to change their rites, customs and habits unless they are most openly opposed to religion and good morals. For what can be more absurd than to transport France, Spain or Italy or any other part of Europe to China? It is not these but faith you should carry, which neither repudiates, nor injures any nation's rites and customs provided they are not evil but rather wishes that they remain intact."[11] Nothing can be clearer, nothing more forceful.

Coming nearer to our own time, we find the same unbroken line in the application of the principle continued by Pope Pius XII of immortal memory when he says: "The Church from the beginning down to our own time has followed this wise practice: let not the Gospel on being introduced into any new land destroy or extinguish whatever its people possess that is naturally good, just or beautiful. For the Church when she calls people to a higher culture and a better way of life, under the inspiration of the Christian religion, does not act like one who recklessly cuts down and uproots a thriving forest. No, she grafts a good scion upon the wild stock that it may bear a crop of more delicious fruit."[12]

From the texts quoted above, it is clear that the preacher's task is twofold: first, he must make an accurate study of the cultural heritage of the people to be evangelized—he must know the value of what the people possess; secondly, he needs to graft the good scion of the Gospel message upon the stock of the traditional heritage in order that "it may bear a crop of more delicious fruit".

It must be strongly emphasized, however, that adaptation,

[11] *Collectanea Sacrae Congregationis de Propaganda Fide*, I, Rome, 1907, n. 135, p. 42. With regard to the force of the words "apertissime contraria" (most openly opposed) used by the Congregation in this document, Father Semois says that it is useful to emphasize that the force of these words implies absolute certitude and that certitude is not the same as simple possibility or even probability. Cp. Semois, *La Papauté et les Missions*, Louvain 1953 p. 190 (footnote 44). It means, in practice, that where there is doubt the custom must stand.

[12] Pope Pius XII, in Encyclical Letter: "Heralds of the Gospel", June 2, 1951, the Paulist Press edition, p. 25.

as Father Perbal warns,[13] has nothing in common with liberal syncretism which would embrace indistinctly all dogmas, all rites and every superstition in order to make an amalgamation out of them. It is not therefore a question of trying to preserve everything in the traditional religion and cultures of African peoples simply because it is theirs, and trying to foster them side by side with Christianity. It is not an attempt to naturalize the Church so that it might become Nigerian, Chinese, Ghanaian or Indian. The Gospel message must remain the focal point of every missionary activity and must be presented in its full splendour and not weakened in any way but rather adorned, enriched and made more intelligible and attractive by the use of whatever is good, just and beautiful that is found in the cultural heritage of a people.

The Gospel, therefore, must always remain and be made to appear as a message of salvation from God Himself, a message destined for every nation, a way of life which people can and should live while remaining authentic citizens of their own nations.

We shall end this section of our discussion with the most recent pronouncement made by over two thousand dignitaries of the Roman Catholic Church with the Pope at their head, published in the *Dogmatic Constitution on the Church* issued during the Second Vatican Council: "Since the kingdom of Christ is not of this world (cp. Jn. 18: 36), the Church or People of God in establishing that kingdom takes nothing away from the temporal welfare of any people. Rather does it foster and take to itself, in so far as they are good, the ability, riches and customs in which the genius of each expresses itself. Taking them to itself it purifies, strengthens, elevates and consecrates them."[14]

---

[13] Cp. A. Perbal, "Les vertus des païens et la tradition missionnaire", in *Bulletin des Missions*, 2 (1938) 93; also J. Champagne, *Manuel d'action missionnaire*, Ottawa, 1947, p. 606: "Quant au message lui-même, le principe d'adaptation ne veut pas dire qu'il doive être incomplet, tronqué ou frelaté. . . . La vérité certes doit être presentée tout entière et dans toute sa splendeur, mais dosée graduellement à la capacité de chacun."

[14] Second Vatican Council, *Dogmatic Constitution on the Church* (De Ecclesia), Rome, November 21, 1964, Art. 13, the Catholic Truth Society of Ireland edition, p. 21. Cp. also Cardinal L. Rugambwa, "The Role of Catholicism in Africa", in *College Readings on Africa*, Cincinnati, 1963, p. 77: "His [church's] mission includes the task of perfecting, spiritualizing whatever is naturally good in African culture, so that it becomes a help to the people in saving their souls." In the light

II. GOD, SPIRITS AND THE SPIRIT WORLD

I should like to approach this subject from the point of view of the Igbo-speaking people of Eastern Nigeria. It is necessary to limit the field because there are so many local peculiarities in the traditonal religion of Africa that it would be impossible to discuss, within the compass of this paper, the whole of Africa in some detail and with any degree of accuracy. There are, nevertheless, some fundamental elements of belief which are of extensive application; among these are the Supreme Being, minor divinities, ancestors and life after death.

In dealing with the African who has not been influenced notably by the Western culture in his traditional environment, we must bear in mind that we are dealing with one for whom the traditional heritage has the force of law. His most important reason for believing what he believes and doing what he does is that it was handed down to him: his father and his grandfather believed and practised those things, and any deviation would be calling for trouble from the invisible world. It is this unshakeable faith in the tradition handed down that explains the baffling ignorance exhibited by those questioned when scholars try to find out the why and the wherefore of most of the things the African believes and practises.

(a) The Spirit World in General

In the world of spirits, Africans distinguish four main categories of spiritual beings: the Supreme God, a multitude of lesser divinities and spirits, the ancestral spirits, and evil spirits. In his book, *Bishop Shanahan of Southern Nigeria*, Father Jordan writes: "The average native was admirably suited by environment and training for an explanation of life in terms of spirit rather than of the flesh. He was no materialist. Indeed nothing was farther from his mind than a materialistic philosophy of existence. It made no appeal to him."[15] For the African, the

of the above, this statement of Father Alves about the progress of the Church in Angola cannot be justified: "Ainsi l'Angola est en train de devenir de plus en plus chrétien et portugais"; P. H. Alves, C.S.Sp., in "Annales Spiritaines", 7 (1954), 108.

[15] J. Jordan, C.S.Sp., *Bishop Shanahan of Southern Nigeria*, Dublin, Clonmore and Reynolds Ltd., 1948, p. 124; cp. also E. G. Parrinder, *African Traditional Religion*, London, Hutchinson, 1954, pp. 20–28.

world of spirits is a real world. It is conceived by the Igbo as a distinct world in itself. It has, however, the closest possible relationship with this material world. It is the spiritual beings which actually control the world; indeed, the world is a spiritual arena in which the various categories of spiritual beings display their powers. Man, in particular, is entirely dependent upon these spiritual beings.

The world of men and the world of spirits are not two independent worlds; for one has no meaning without the other—they are complementary. Man has need of the spirit-world, while the minor spirits have need of men to gladden their hearts, to feed them with fat things. It must be pointed out, however, that between the world of men directed by the spirits and the spirit-world, there reigns order, not chaos. The spirits can topple the order of the world as a punishment for man's offences, but man has ways and means of preventing this or restoring the order when upset. On this Westermann writes: "The world of the African is characterised by its unity and coherence . . . and a correct understanding [of African life] can only be obtained by surveying life as a whole."[16]

(b) *The Supreme God (Chukwu or Chineke)*

In his paper entitled *God*, Professor Idowu has treated this topic in some detail. We intend to discuss the Supreme God cult as known among the Igbo, with a view to throwing some light on certain matters about which there are misconceptions, such as the "absence of cult" so often sponsored by writers on African religion.

It is a fact that belief in a Supreme Being is universal among the Igbo people, and though various names are used to designate him in different areas, yet the reality which those names try to express is essentially the same. Is he worshipped? If so, to what extent?

Basden remarks that "although there is a universal belief in a Supreme Being and his inveterate enemy the Devil, the *effect* of such a belief is negligible. It is purely theoretical and has no

[16] D. Westermann, *The African Today and Tomorrow*, London, O.U.P., 1949, p. 83.

marked influence on life or character."[17] Other writers have made similar observations. Unegbu observes that ". . . the strange thing was that while the place was full of idols; while an altar of worship was dedicated to any god that claimed to exercise some influence over man, there was none to the 'Unknown God' of the Greeks or the 'Great God' of the Ibos."[18] It is our considered opinion, however, that such views do not do justice to the facts; a more careful study of Igbo religion shows that the Supreme Being is not as "unknown" as he is thought to be.

(1) Indirect Cult

Regular sacrifices and prayers are offered to the minor divinities such as *Ana* (earth goddess), *Udo*, *Eke*, *Ogwugwu*. During these sacrifices, God may be mentioned and his help invoked explicitly. Sometimes he is not mentioned at all; but whether he is mentioned or not, he is generally believed to be the "ultimate recipient of offerings to lesser gods, who may be explicitly referred to as intermediaries".[19] Homage is most commonly paid to God through his most powerful agents the Sun (*Anyanwu*) and Thunder (*Amadioha*). Some, in fact, identify God with the Sun, but the majority maintain that they worship him through the Sun and regard the Sun as God's son; hence the saying, *Anyanwu bu Nwa Chukwu*, the Sun is God's son. The cult of *Amadioha* as an agent of the Supreme God is widespread in Owerri. Sometimes God is called upon to arbitrate through his agent *Amadioha* in land cases, and in disputes involving false and malicious accusations. The ritual is simple. A white cock is taken to the shrine of *Amadioha*, tied to a bamboo stick which is then stuck in the ground before the shrine. The offender is asked to declare his innocence and then to break an egg before the shrine of *Amadioha*; this part of the ritual is called *itu-ogu*. If he is innocent, it is believed that thunder and lightning will

---

[17] G. T. Basden, *Niger Ibos*, London, Seeley Service, 1938, p. 37. *Ibid.*: "As he is *not* honoured with an 'Alusi', neither is sacrifice ever made directly to appease him."

[18] M. Unegbu, "Ibos and Christianity", in *Missionary Annals* 2 (1954), 12; cp. also C. K. Meek, "The Religions of Nigeria", in *Africa* 3 (1943), 112–113: "But he is a distant God of vague personality and sacrifice is seldom offered to him directly."

[19] D. Forde and G. I. Jones, *The Ibo and Ibibio-Speaking Peoples of South-Eastern Nigeria*, London, International African Institute, 1962, p. 25.

fight his cause. The head of the cock is torn off the body and placed at the shrine. The Supreme God is expected to act unfailingly through his agent.

In Okpatu in Udi Division, there are shrines called *Onuanyanwu*, literally the Sun's month. The component parts of such a shrine are: pieces of stones, *ofor* (the symbol of justice and an essential cult object of the Igbo), *Ogbu* tree, woven palm-frond, one small earthenware pot which must not be painted in any way; it must be free of any artificially applied colour (the people describe its colour as "white"). Rites are performed, during which the people say: "We offer sacrifice to *Anyanwu* and we ask him to present it to God." A similar cult obtains in the neighbouring town of Ukana. In Agulu in Awka Division, the most powerful local deity is *Ududonka*. *Ududonka* is a famous male deity and the people hold that they offer sacrifice to God through this local agent.

(2) *Direct Cult*

God is often invoked first, before the minor gods, when offerings are being made. The following is an example of a common formula for offering kola-nut:[20]

Chukwu taa oji	God, eat kola-nut
muo taanu oji	spirits, eat kola-nut
igwe taa oji	sky, eat kola-nut
Agbala taa oji	Agbala (one of the minor divinities) eat kola-nut
ayi aya anwu	may we not die
ayi aya efu	may we not perish
ekwena k'anyi yaa	may we not be sick
ekwena k'anyi dudue	may we not be tormented with maladies.

Another example of prayer addressed directly to God is the following recorded from an elderly pagan of Ukana:

Chineke kelu mmadu!	God who created man!
Ndum, ndu ndi nkem	My life, the lives of my relatives

[20] This was the morning prayer of a Nnewi priest while offering kola-nut.

onye sim di, nya di	Whoever wishes me to live, let him live also
onye sim nwuhu, nya nwuhu	Whoever wishes me to die, let him die
onye sim nweta, nweta	Whoever wishes that I should have good things, let him have them
onye sim elina, onu kpoluya nku	Whoever says that I should not eat, let his mouth dry up.

In parts of Nsukka Division, the cult of the Supreme Being is fairly widespread. Almost every home in Okpuje, Aro-Uno, Oba and in many other villages has an altar dedicated to *Ezechitoke*.[21] These shrines usually consist of a few flat stones, with two bamboo sticks fixed some two feet apart and a strip of cloth stretching across, tied to the ends of the sticks. From this strip of cloth hang smaller strips of various colours, with white predominating. Offerings of kola-nuts, food and fowls are made to *Ezechitoke* on this spot. Prayers are made as accompaniment to the presentation skywards of the gifts to *Ezechitoke* who is asked, in company with other spirits, to accept the gifts. Here is an example of the formula used by the priest of Okpuje:

Ezechitoke, Ana, Ugwuokpuje mulum,	Ezechitoke, Earth deity, Ugwuokpuje (hill deity) that gave me birth
nyem ife olili	give me things to eat
nyem omumu	give me offspring
nyem nwanyi	give me wives
nyem ego	give me money
gozie madu nine	bless all men.

In addition, the people of Okpuje have an annual feast in honour of *Ezechitoke*. This feast is termed *Ili agba Chukwu*, that is, "eating the covenant of God", and it is celebrated during the yam festival.

Perhaps a more significant and more widespread form of

---

[21] *Ezechitoke* is the name used by the elders for the Supreme God in parts of Nsukka Division. Nowadays, *Chukwu* or *Chineke* is more commonly used all over Igbo-land, mainly as a result of the influence of schools and Christianity. *Ezechitoke* is rapidly falling out of use. It only survives among the elders.

sacrifice to the High God is the *Aja Eze-enu*, "the sacrifice to the King of the sky", which is of frequent occurrence in Awgu Division and in parts of Awka, Onitsha, and Afikpo. The main elements of this sacrifice are a bamboo stick which can be of any length between ten and thirty feet, one white cock, a strip of white cloth, some leaves of *ebenebe* tree, some kola-nuts and, in places like Afikpo, some seed-yams. The cock is not killed but tied to one end of the stick; the strip of cloth and the *ebenebe* leaves are also fastened to the stick, which is then fixed upright in the ground. Where seed-yams are used they may also be attached to the bamboo stick. The kola-nuts are left at the foot of the stick. This sacrifice may be offered in front of a person's compound or within the precincts of a deity. Nothing used for this sacrifice may be eaten. The priest who offers it may be paid for his services with a few cups of wine. An adult may offer the sacrifice on behalf of himself and his family, but no female may set it up. When there is a bad harvest, or a serious sickness, or an accident, or a calamity—that is, when someone is in trouble or in need of some help which he feels cannot be supplied by man—then a diviner prescribes a sacrifice to *Eze-enu*. This sacrifice is offered just at sunrise.

There is another type of direct sacrifice which one comes across occasionally. This type is not offered at any special shrine, since in many parts of Igbo land God has no recognized place where sacrifice is offered to him. Such a sacrifice was witnessed in Ihe in Awgu Division. The relatives of a young girl, who was about to get married, consulted a diviner and were told that a sacrifice had to be offered to God for the success of the proposed marriage. A priest at the shrine of *Ana-Ihe*,[22] a relative of the prospective bride, was requested to offer the sacrifice. The principal elements of the sacrifice were a cock, some large yams and boat-shaped receptacles woven from palm-frond. The sacrifice was offered within the *Ana-Ihe* square, but not before any shrine, even though there were at least ten minor shrines within the square. The priest, seated on his traditional stool in the open and surrounded by the clients, offered the cock and then killed it, sprinkling the blood over the receptacles; yams were peeled and boiled and a meal prepared. The following prayer was addressed to God by the priest:

[22] *Ana-Ihe* is the principal earth deity of Ihe, a town in Awgu Division.

God, who created man, behold this fowl! God, who created man, behold Ugwuaku (the prospective bride) my child; protect her for me. Offspring is the main thing in the world. God, who acts according to his designs, give her children. Preserve her husband-to-be. Give him the means of giving me wealth to eat. If she gives birth to a female child, it will live, if a male, it will live. May she not have difficulties in child-birth. May her health be good; may the health of her future husband be good. Prayer obtains both among the spirits and among men. God, treat me well! I am asking for goodness. My son-in-law shall give me things and I shall eat. Love will exist between us. God, that is what I ask for. Ihe land! Spirits of Ihe! God the Creator! I thank you. I have finished.[23]

When it was suggested to the priest in question that he might have borrowed his ideas about the High God from Christians, he retorted immediately and emphatically: *Chineke dili be anyi duduludu;*[24] *anyi na akpalu Ya Ugbo* (God has been among us from time immemorial; we weave sacrificial boat for him).[25]

It is evident from the above that God is worshipped in many parts of Igbo land. Though there are no images or statues representative of the Supreme God, yet there are specific offerings to him, such offerings varying in frequency from place to place.

(c) *The Minor Divinities and other Spirits*

It is commonly believed among the Igbos that the Supreme Being has created the minor divinities as agents. There are multitudes of these spirits of different ranks, charged with specific functions for man and society. Some of these divinities are recognized by all villages and families, and they perform the same functions for men. Some of them are household gods. "The most universal of these household gods, and that which is given first rank, is the Ikenga, and no house may be without one. It is the first god sought by a young man at the beginning of his career, and it is the one to which he looks for good luck in all

[23] This formula was tape-recorded in the vernacular and translated almost literally.

[24] *Duduludu* means from time immemorial. I cannot think of any other word that brings out more clearly and forcefully the fact that what the priest has just done is altogether indigenous and as old as the town itself.

[25] Sacrificial boat is a boat-shaped receptacle prepared from palm-frond and used for holding part of the victims for sacrifice. To weave sacrificial boat is simply another way of saying that sacrifice is offered.

his enterprises."[26] The Land (*Ana* or *Ale* or *Ala*) is another prominent deity among the Igbo, and is regarded as the queen of
the underworld. "She is the source and judge of human morality and accordingly exercises the main ritual sanctions in disputes and offences. . . . Laws are made and oaths are sworn
in her name. . . . A shrine for Ale rituals is found in each village."[27]

The point has been made that these spirits are agents of the
Supreme God; actually, this is so more in theory than in practice. These spirits, it appears, are self-sufficient and do not
therefore have to receive gifts from the Supreme God in order
to distribute such to humans. They can bestow these gifts *of
themselves*, thereby acting independently of the Supreme God.
The position, therefore, in actual practice, seems to be like this:
God created these spirits and assigned them their special
responsibilities and areas of jurisdiction. They have their resources and have full powers to act without consulting God or
asking for his permission. They, unlike the Supreme God, can
sometimes disappoint man; this is why both success and failures
are attributed to them. Like the Greek gods of old, they have
some of the limitations of man. They can be hungry, angry,
jealous and revengeful. In view of this, man must always seek
to be on the best of terms with them.[28]

Some of these deities are male, others female, and each is
represented accordingly. To these deities are brought different kinds of offerings and sacrifices according to the express
demands of each particular divinity. The devotees salute, bow,
genuflect and prostrate as appropriate as they pass their shrines.
Women, in particular, and indeed all those who are setting
off on a journey, ask for the protection of any divinities they
may pass on the way. It must be emphasized, however, that
"the Ibo does not bow down to wood and stone. He bows down
to the indwelling spirit only and therefore troubles little about

[26] G. T. Basden, *Among the Ibos of Nigeria*, London, Seeley Service and Company
Ltd., 1921, p. 219.

[27] Forde and Jones, *op. cit.*, p. 25.

[28] Cp. J. Jordan, *op. cit.*, p. 126: "Every Ibo believed that an invisible universe
was in action all around him and that his term of life was short if he happened to
fall foul of its denizens. He felt that it was up to him to propitiate them and to
treat them with courtesy and deference. That was the fundamental reason why he
had such a penchant for sacrifice in all its various forms."

42

the outer husk".[29] In fact, "no Ibo would for a moment have credited a material thing with a spiritual power *a se*; it could never be more than a receptacle for a spirit which worked through it".[30]

In addition to these minor divinities, the Igbo people "believe that every human being has a genius or spiritual double known as his *chi* which is associated with him from the moment of conception, to which his abilities, faults and good or bad fortune are ascribed, and into whose care is entrusted the fulfilment of the destiny which *Chuku* has prescribed. After marriage or the birth of a child a person establishes a cult for his or her *chi*, building a shrine at which sacrifices for assistance in achieving desired ends are offered."[31] This belief in a protecting spirit is found in other parts of Africa. The LoDagaa of West Africa have a tutelary spirit both for the individual and for the clan.

(d) *Ancestral Spirits*

Among the good spirits are the ancestors. Their cult is of supreme importance in the life of the African. Space limits exhaustive treatment of this subject, but it must be stated that, to the older African men and women in the hinterland villages, life from day to day—and we might legitimately say from moment to moment—has no meaning at all apart from ancestral presence and power. The father of a family begins the day by praying to them, dedicating himself and his entire family to their protection, offering kola-nuts, and also palm wine when available.

Apart from this daily offering, there is the annual feast in honour of the ancestors. On this occasion every adult, male and female, offers something (usually fowls) to ancestors now dwelling in the other world. There are also sacrifices offered whenever the ancestors so demand. This may happen when a member

[29] S. Leith-Ross, *African Women. A Study of the Ibo of Nigeria*, London, Faber, 1934, p. 120.

[30] Jordan, *op. cit.*, p. 124; Wilhelm Schmidt, S.V.D., *The Origin and Growth of Religion: Facts and Theories*. Translated by H. J. Rose, London, Methuen and Company Ltd., 1931, pp. 59–60: "But above all, there is not a single religion, even in West Africa, the strong-hold of fetishism, which consists of fetishism wholly or even principally."

[31] Forde and Jones, *op. cit.*, p. 26.

of the family is ill or some calamity has befallen the family. The diviner prescribes the type of sacrifice demanded by the ancestors if the latter are responsible for the sickness or calamity.

The ancestors are in such close relationship with the people that in some parts of Igbo land it is forbidden not to reserve some food in the pots during supper lest the ancestors come and find the pots empty. They are most welcome in the families when they reincarnate and begin to live among their own again.

(e) *Evil Spirits*

In addition to the good spirits discussed above, evil spirits also abound. The *Eshu* among the Yoruba, and the *Ekwensu*[32] or *Akalogeli* among the Igbo, are evil spirits; however, unlike the *Ekwensu*, the *Eshu* can be employed for a good end as well. Among the Igbo, everything about the nature of these spirits, apart from their work, is shrouded in mystery. Whenever it is known that they are causing trouble, a special offering known as *ichu-aja* is made to them. The pagan makes this offering to these "spirits shrouded in mystery whom he cannot manage, and whom he holds responsible for his present sickness or other trouble. He cannot locate the spirits; he has no conception how or why they persecute him, yet he is convinced that they are the authors of all the evils that overtake him. In his distress he consults the *dibia* (medicine-man) and, acting on his advice, endeavours to appease the spirits by performing inchu-aja, lit. to drive evil."[33] What is offered is always something that is of little or no use for human life, unlike that which is given to good spirits; such materials include strips of old cloth, a lizard, a toad, rotten eggs, broken cowries, etc.

The end is not to make friends with, but to drive away, the evil spirits. The person who carries this offering to give to the spirits walks in dead silence, and neither salutes nor responds to salutation until he has deposited the offering at the designated place, usually at a crossroads.

[32] In some parts of Igbo land like Oraeri, *Ekwensu* is regarded as one of the good spirits. In this particular town, Oraeri, *Akalogeli* is the word used to denote the evil spirits.

[33] G. T. Basden, *op. cit.*, p. 224.

III. PRACTICAL APPLICATION

What has been said above is only an introduction to the subject under discussion. For successful evangelization, a more thorough knowledge is necessary. It is clear that the Igbo traditional religion has prepared fertile ground for Christianity, and it is no wonder that Christianity does thrive. Prudence and patience are needed for successful adaptation; that is why the Sacred Congregation for the Propagation of the Faith warns missionaries to handle religious problems carefully and in a painstaking manner.[34] Equipped with sound principles, the man on the spot, who has to take into consideration various local matters, is entrusted with the actual application of the principles in question.

It would be wise, for example, to apply African sayings about God to the God of the Bible. The missionary must also be sure that he is employing the right name for God. Such a procedure could open religious springs which were almost blocked up. The teaching on divine providence is very positive and practical and will surely appeal to the Igbo. A new horizon will open to them. God should be seen more as a *loving Father* than as one to be feared; pagan religion emphasizes fear rather than love. Africans should be made to realize that God "is not far from each one of us, for 'In him we live and move and have our being.' For we are indeed his offspring."[35]

Belief in Angels replaces belief in minor divinities without much difficulty. Ancestral cult prepares the ground for the doctrine of the Communion of Saints. The strong attachment to ancestors makes it easy to promote both devotion to the Saints and prayers for the departed ones. In the light of the first and second burials,[36] Month's Mind and anniversary services could be used, though not without some difficulty, to correct some practices that run counter to the faith in the second burial ceremonies.

[34] Cf. *Monita ad Missionarios, Sacrae Congregationis de Propaganda Fide*, Rome, 1950, ch. iv., art. 4.

[35] *Acts* 17:28.

[36] Cp. J. Jordan, *op. cit.*, p. 132: "Every pagan has two burials, one for the body immediately after death and the second and more important for the soul, after some weeks or even longer." The people believe that until all the ceremonies of the second burial are duly performed on behalf of the dead his spirit remains a homeless wanderer not yet qualified for admission to the place of rest and enjoyment.

Bishop Whelan recommends that the belief in guardian angels should be made to replace that in the protecting spirit *chi*.[37] We would go further than that: in prayers, the word *chi* should be retained in the same way that the pagan God-name *Chukwu* has smoothly passed into Christian usage. Of course, the people would have to be made to realize, contrary to Igbo belief, that misfortune is not the work of the *chi*.

With regard to the use of images, there should be no difficulty from the point of view of those Christian denominations like the Roman Catholics. It is necessary, however, that their use should be properly explained so that the people do not fall into idolatry by worshipping instead of venerating them.

While we affirm the existence and power of evil spirits, yet we must guard against the exaggeration of their presence and influence. It is clear that most of the incidents attributed to evil powers in the day-to-day lives of the people could be avoided or neutralized as to their effects by education or the observance of the laws of hygiene; hence the importance of education. "Thorough investigation first" should be the watchword in dealing with most of the supposed instances of the influence of the evil spirits.

Conclusion

Generally speaking, very little has been done in the actual work of understanding the traditional religion of Africa. There are parts of the continent which have scarcely been studied at all.

It is necessary, therefore, that all scholars, teachers and heralds of the Gospel should co-operate actively in this task of seeking to understand the essence of African religion. We are convinced that there are in African life and thought hidden treasures, precious gems, provided by God for the embellishment of the Gospel. The present generation has inherited a precious tradition from its forbears—a tradition that puts God first in everything, a tradition in which the spiritual takes precedence over the material.

It is the privileged responsibility of preachers to identify the gems, remove the dross where such exists, and build on a lasting foundation.

[37] Cp. J. B. Whelan, "The Ten Commandments" in *The Herald*, 293 (1945), 8.

3

PRIESTHOOD

N̄ganga is the commonest and most widely used word for "priest" in the Congolese cultural context. It is sometimes found in the form *N̄gaa* or *Ga*. The same term may be found elsewhere in the Bantu world, as is the case with such words as *Muntu* (man, person) and *N̄zambi* (God).

Our paper will be mainly concerned with Congolese priesthood and its confrontation with Biblical revelation.

At the present time, many men bear the name *N̄ganga*. This fact belongs to the sphere of *mukisi* (fetish; pl. *mikisi*). In Congolese tradition, there are in fact three things which are taken into consideration in choosing the name of a child:

1. *The mukisi.* If, during the mother's pregnancy, she has been treated with the *mukisi* called *Kilonda*, or if the child himself has been treated with this *mukisi*, it will be called *Mukanza*. Many present-day proper names derive from the *mikisi*.

2. The answer given to someone, or the way in which one reacts to particular circumstances. In my clan, there was someone who interfered in matters which he did not begin to understand. In order to condemn this kind of behaviour, I was given the name *Buana* (meet, happen). If today many Congolese have the name *N̄ganga*, it is because the *nganga* had been called upon repeatedly to save the lives of these Congolese. The word is also used as a proper name in order to protect one's child against evil.

3. The memory of someone departed. If a member of the clan who was called *N̄ganga* has disappeared, the same name will be given to one of the children of the clan in

47

memory of the departed. In this way, a name which at first had a religious meaning will simply be handed on from generation to generation.

The word *Nganga* is closely linked with the *mikisi*. Each *mukisi* is linked with a *nganga*, who is usually a man and sometimes a woman. People may say: *Ngang'a ngombo* (i.e. the priest of the fetish called *ngombo*), *ngang'a lemba* (the priest of the fetish called *lemba*). There is no *nganga* without a *mukisi* and there is no *mukisi* without a *nganga*. This close relationship between *nganga* and *mukisi* seems to be at the root of the word *bunganga* (fetish) or *manganga* (fetishes). *Nganga* may have been at the origin a *mukisi*.

After these few remarks on the term *nganga*, let us turn to our subject itself.

I. CONGOLESE PRIESTHOOD

We have translated *nganga* as "priest". This translation seems to suggest that *nganga* places himself as a mediator between *Nzambi* and *Muntu*. On the contrary, *Nzambi*, who is all-powerful, eternal and unconfined, has created *Muntu*, but withdrew because of a mistake which *Muntu* committed. Thereafter, *Muntu* is mercilessly subjected to evil which manifests itself in particular as illness and death. We see immediately that it is the problem of evil which led *Muntu* to found the priesthood. According to the Bantu mentality in general and the Congolese mentality in particular, evil has six causes:

1. *Nzambi*. One saying goes, *Nzambi bubote wa tusidi, kaa ga kati wizi tula bubi* (God, you have been good to us, but you have put evil among us). The evil in question is death. It is generally agreed that the death of old people is caused by God.
2. *Ndoki* (sorcerer). It is said, *Mu Nzambi na Nzambi nga babingi tuena, bandoki ba tumeni* (If it were only God, we should be many; it is the sorcerers who destroy us). *Ndoki* can and must be translated "destroyer of the soul", soul being understood as the inner man.
3. *Mukuyu* (ghost). After death *ndoki* becomes *mukuyu* (pl. *mikuyu*). The *mikuyu* are shut out of the "Congolese paradise" called the "village of ripe bananas". They give themselves up to the service of the *bandoki* (sorcerers), and generally undergo the second death.

48

4. *An angry Mukuya.* After death, *Muntu* who was not a *ndoki* becomes *mukuya* (the good spirit of the dead; pl. *mikuya*). The *mikuya* may live either in paradise or in the village of the living, in little huts called *nsinda* (temple for the ancestral spirits).

5. *Mukisi.* Paradoxically, the *Mukisi* who is used to fight evil may itself be a source of evil. For example, if evil is caused by the fetish *Kinene*, it must be fought by the same fetish.

6. *A moral offence.* A woman who has committed adultery suffers when she gives birth. She is forced to denounce the man with whom she has committed the evil. In other words, she must make public confession of her fault.

Nganga never places himself as a mandated mediator between man and God, so that God may intervene to destroy the evil. On the contrary, *nganga* takes no account of evil caused by God, and interposes himself only between man and all the other agents of evil, viz. *ndoki, mukuyu, mukuya* and *mukisi.*

Let us go back for a moment to the word *ndoki.* We have already said that *ndoki* is the destroyer of the real man (i.e. the inner man, as distinguished from the visible or physical man). A man who is destroyed by *ndoki* may go on living physically for some time, but in the end he succumbs, because his real being has left him. The technical expression for the mysterious operation of *ndoki* is *dia muntu* (to eat the man, to destroy the man's real being). To carry out this destructive work, the *ndoki* possesses two weapons: the *mukuyu* and *kundu*. We already know what *mukuyu* is. Let us look for a moment at the *kundu*. *Kundu* is the organ by which *ndoki* does his work. This organ is an integral part of his being. Some think that *kundu* is more precisely the stomach. Whatever its physical or metaphysical nature, *kundu* is considered to be the main cause of evil, in particular of illness and death. The *kundu* is usually acquired by initiation, but it may be acquired by heredity or by accident. There is no *ndoki* without *kundu* and there is no *kundu* without *ndoki*.

The *kundu* is thus a cause of *ndoki* and *mukuyu*. The ordinary man (*muntu wa mpamba*) has no power on *ndoki* and *mukuyu*. He cannot protect himself against these two enemies. Only *nganga* can denounce and destroy them; only he can interpose himself between the ordinary man and the two evildoers, to reduce them to nothing. Nor has the ordinary man any authority over the angry *mukuya*. Once more, it is *nganga* who has the

49

power to appease him. The work of *nganga* is not limited to the destruction of *ndoki* and *mukuyu* or the appeasing of *mukuya's* anger. On the contrary, it seems to include other spheres of activity. *Nganga* can be the only power concerned with the healing of the sick; the *ndoki*, the *mukuyu* or the angry *mukuya* may not intervene at all. In this case, he looks for or makes medicines from metals, plants or animals. From this point of view, *nganga* seems to us to act as a chemist or a doctor.

As *nganga* is called to fight the power of both physical and metaphysical evil, he practises magic. He claims to act both on objects and on events. He gives the impression of cutting off his tongue, swallowing a flame of fire, or plunging a sharp knife in his belly without hurting himself. *Nganga* therefore gains the reputation of being a remarkable magician.

Finally, *nganga* appears to us to act as a prophet or visionary. He claims to have the ability to unfold the secrets of the heart or, when he goes into ecstasy, to foretell the future. He plays a part in the political, social and economic spheres: he confers authority on the village chief, encourages fertility, blesses every undertaking. He is undoubtedly the most powerful, influential and complex figure in Congolese society. That is why the word *nganga* may be translated priest, chemist, doctor, magician, prophet and visionary.

When we ask the question: "From whom does *nganga* get his power?" the opinion of the elders is twofold. Some maintain that *nganga* receives his power from *Nzambi*. The others, however, claim that it is the *mikuya* who grant power to the *nganga*. Whatever answer is given, *nganga's* authority does not come either from himself or from the living. He derives it from the metaphysical world.

Let us see now how *nganga* acts when he is called upon in a particular case. In case of illness, death or any other abnormal situation, the main concern is to discover the cause of the evil. To this end, a *ngang'a ngombo* (priest specialized in discovering causes) is called in. *Ngang'a ngombo* finds out the cause of the evil and indicates which *nganga* should be called upon to destroy the evil. The *nganga* in charge of the case organizes one or more cultic gatherings at which he gives himself up to dancing, ecstasy, singing, and all kinds of gestures which tend to make him both indispensable and terrifying. Within the sound and sight of everyone, *nganga* uses his *mukisi*, the concrete symbol of which is a parcel (*futu*) containing either an idol, or a variety of more or less strange objects. There is no *mukisi* without a material support. But unknown to the audience, *nganga* claims to be sustained by the *mikuya* (the spirits of the ancestors favourable to the life of the clan). It is also agreed that the *nganga* may work together with God. Guaranteed in this way by the metaphysical world, and acting through material objects, *nganga* throws himself into the struggle against evil, sure of coming out of it triumphant. It is generally believed that he destroys the *ndoki* and the *mukuyu*, and effectively appeases *mukuya's* anger.

When it is a question of "killing" the *mukyu*, *nganga* orders the corpse to be burned, or else he pretends to burn it by firing a gun. Before "dying", the *mukuyu* is believed to cry: *Mfwidi mfwa zole* (I am dying a second time).

If there is a sick person to be cared for, the *nganga* will treat him directly with the *mukusi*, and will forbid him to do all kinds of things. These prohibitions may be either alimentary or moral. The effectiveness of certain *mikisi* depends on the *nganga* treating the patient in a sort of temporary "convent" called *Vuela*. The *Vuela* hut is built in some areas on the edge of the village, in other areas in the middle. The patients are not simply treated in the *Vuela*; they are initiated, while they are there, into the fetish used by the *nganga*.

In many ceremonies, *nganga* appeases the angry *mikuya* by bloody sacrifices which are normally cocks, hens and goats. The blood is given to the ancestral spirits, while the meat is eaten by *nganga*, the patient and the participants.

Once the ceremony is over, *nganga* goes home, after receiving his remuneration in the form of food, an animal, poultry or money. Thus, the Congolese priest works both for his own living and for the life of his clientele.

What were the immediate or mediate consequences of the *nganga's* activity in the old Congolese society? Three points are worth underlining. In the first place, the *nganga*, by fighting against illnesses, contributed to the development of medicine. Many sick people recovered their health because of his intervention. Unfortunately, Westerners have harmed this kind of medicine because they were unable to analyse *nganga's* activities in sufficient depth. In the second place, *nganga* founded and strengthened the idea of authority in Congolese society, and perhaps in the African world as a whole. It was from him that in olden days the politician drew his power. *Nganga* does not give orders, but without him political, social and even juridical authority is in danger of crumbling. In the third place, *nganga*, in particular *ngang'a ngombo*, contributed to the break-up of Congolese society. Clans were divided into several fragments, which were at odds with each other because the *ngang'a ngombo*, or simply the *nganga*, denounced the *ndoki* arbitrarily and falsely. As, within each clan, there are several matriarchal and patriarchal lines of descent, the sick or dead man's line rises against the line of the member who has been denounced. In the end, under the influence of hatred or fear, the members of one clan who had been united are divided into two opposing camps and separate for good. Without the *nganga* the belief in *kundu* (sorcery) would not be deeply rooted in the Congolese soul.

But the *nganga's* influence is not confined to society in the olden days. For good or ill, Christianity has not always escaped the heritage of *nganga*. The Christian missionary (minister, priest or Salvation Army officer) drew part of his authority, without knowing it, from the psychological state which *nganga* had created. The missionary was called *ngang'a Nzambi* (God's priest), as distinct from the *ngang'a mukisi* (the fetish priest). It goes without saying that the missionary benefited from the respect which was formerly due to the *ngang'a mukisi*. Not only the *nganga's Nzambi* was respected, but because of the colour of his skin, his technique and his science, he was feared far too much. *Ngang'a Nzambi* was considered infinitely superior to the *ngang'a mukisi*. It is also generally agreed that Catholic priests have the power of capturing the *mikuyu* (ghosts) and carrying off the *mikuya* (the good spirits of the dead). Protestant missionaries have not always escaped the effects of this superstition. Noticing that these missionaries laid flowers beside the grave of one of their departed colleagues, people wondered whether they did not enter into direct relationship with the spirits of the dead. The Congolese priest or minister is also called *ngang'a Nzambi*. He profits from the situation created by *nganga* and the *missionary*. *Nganga* has not only assured to some extent the social status of Church workers; he has also left them the legacy of religious and moral conceptual tools. It is undoubtedly *nganga* who created words such as *Nzambi* (God), *sumuka* (to defile oneself; hence *masumu*, sin), *nlongo* or *tsina* (saint; hence *bunlongo*, holiness and *kinlongo*, temple), *lusemo* (blessing; hence *sakumuna* = to bless), *bieka*, *tumba* (consecrate; hence *mbiekolo*, consecration), *lulendo* (power) etc. *Nganga's* work partly enabled the Bible to be translated into Congolese languages. The Christian preacher consciously or unconsciously uses part of the vocabulary left by *nganga*. This is where Congolese priesthood confronts Biblical revelation.

II. CONGOLESE PRIESTHOOD AND BIBLICAL REVELATION

We do not intend to go deeply into Biblical priesthood in order to compare it with Congolese priesthood. We shall simply underline the essential and fundamental aspect of Biblical priesthood, in order to determine our attitude to Congolese priesthood.

The priest (*cohen*), or the high priest in the Old Testament, is from the beginning the mediator between the chosen but sinful people on the one hand and God on the other hand. All one need do is to read carefully the first five chapters of Leviticus. In this passage the priest is the duly authorized mediator between God and man. When man wishes to enter into any kind of relationship with God it is the priest, the appointed specialist, who comes between the two parties.

The Old Testament priest derives his authority from God (Ex. 28: 1, 36; Deut. 33: 10), never from the spirits of the dead (the law expressly forbids any relationship with the dead, Deut. 18: 10–11; cf. 1 Sam. 28: 6–25). Although the priest sometimes used the urim and thummim (Num. 27: 21; 1 Sam. 14: 36 f.), objects which might be compared with the *mikisi*, yet his work is not to denounce the *ndoki*, or transmit the will of the dead. Instead, he offers himself as an instrument of the will of God.

In the New Testament, Christ is presented to us as the High Priest of the New Covenant. It is unnecessary to point out that it is the author of the Epistle to the Hebrews who sees in Christ the fulfilment of the essential and fundamental reality of Old

Testament priesthood. The author develops this idea especially in chapters 5, 7, 8, 9 and 10. This interpretation of the work of Christ is not conspicuous in Paul, though he seems to be summing up what is said in Hebrews when he writes: "Who shall bring any charge against God's elect? It is God who justifies; who is to condemn? Is it Christ Jesus, who died, yes, who was raised from the dead, who is at the right hand of God, who indeed intercedes for us?" (Rom. 8: 33–34).

By His death, His resurrection and His ascension to the right hand of God, Christ has become the High Priest of all who believe in Him. Like the *cohen* of the Old Testament, Christ is the mediator between God and man—the only mediator. Throughout the New Testament, Christ is not presented to us as the mediator between man and the spirits of the dead. On the contrary, He is the one through whom God wills to reconcile the world to Himself (2 Cor. 5: 18, 19, cp. Col. 1: 19 f.). *Nganga*, in contrast, has no function to fulfil between *Muntu* and *Nzambi* because the former does not sin against the latter, but only against the spirits of the ancestors. *Nzambi* remains more or less neutral in relation to human life. That is why *nganga* places himself as a mediator only between *Muntu* and the dead. However, the activities of *nganga* throw into relief the idea of salvation or deliverance. *Nganga* is certainly the saviour or the liberator of *Muntu*. *Nganga* has undoubtedly contributed to the maintenance of the idea of salvation or deliverance. The desire for salvation or deliverance is fully satisfied by the Son of God, the Saviour and Lord of the World.

It is time for us to define our position in relation to *nganga* in particular and African religion in general, where they are confronted by the revelation in Christ. It is agreed and established once for all that we can neither add to nor take away from the revelation which is Christ Himself, as He is presented to us throughout the Bible. But every time we are asked to make a value judgment on non-Christian religions, on cultures foreign to Biblical revelation, divergences and even diametrically opposed positions come to light. Nor is agreement reached when it is a question of using non-Biblical cultural values. Would it be heresy or theological error if we were to admit, once for all, that Christ, by fulfilling what is positive in the Old Testament, also consummated all religious, social and cultural values which one finds outside the world of the Bible? Of course, it is not a question of canonizing or dogmatizing these values, but in the light of what is said of Christ, we can be first of all convinced that all essential and fundamental values are summed up in Him. "For in him all the fullness of God was pleased to dwell, and through him to reconcile to himself all things, whether on earth or in heaven, making peace by the blood of his cross" (Col. 1: 19–20). The reconciliation which is made by the blood of Christ concerns all the existential realities of every man.

Nganga willed to save man, but did not succeed in doing so; Christ did so fully once for all. Christ has therefore accomplished the work of *Nganga*. Even when one has admitted that Christ has fulfilled not only what is positive in the Old Testament, but also all other possible values, the problem of the use of non-Biblical cultural values is not finally settled. Nor is it because one has found common or contradictory elements in the Bible and in these other values that the problem becomes easy to solve. We must say immediately that the problem cannot be solved once for all, but that it will be asked generation after generation, and will find more or less relative solutions in the perpetual confrontation between Biblical revelation and non-Biblical values. The work of the Holy Spirit enters to some extent into this confrontation by which the Church can and must fulfil its calling in relation to the world and in relation to her Saviour and Lord Jesus Christ. The elements to be used or condemned therefore depend on the sovereign liberty of the Holy Spirit, and on the Church's obedience to the Spirit of Christ.

Our attitude towards *nganga* in particular, and negro-African culture in general, or any other value, is both negative and positive. This double attitude seems to be dictated by revelation itself. Three examples will confirm our thesis.

The first is that of Abraham, called by God to leave his country, his fatherland and his father's house (Gen. 12: 1). But he does not go out alone, stripped of everything. On the contrary, he is accompanied by his wife, his nephew Lot, his servants and his wealth. He leaves "something", and takes "something" with him. Because of God's call, Abraham shows himself both negative and positive in his attitude to his family

55

and wealth. It is this double attitude which enabled him to give a valid answer to God's call.

The second example is provided by Israel's deliverance in Egypt. The people is called to leave the land of bondage, but is also ordered to take with it the wealth it has acquired or will acquire at the last moment (Ex. 12: 29–39). The people leaves "something", takes "something" with it, and will have "something". By acting in this way, Israel will face difficulties inherent in its long vocation. Abraham and Israel do not only leave behind, and take with them, material wealth, but they leave behind and take with them a religious, social and cultural world. This double attitude is dictated and guided by God himself.

The third example is that of Paul speaking to the deeply religious Athenians (Acts 17: 22–34). Here it is not so much a question of leaving behind and taking "something"; it is rather a matter of a point of contact between the Greek religious world and Christ who has died and risen again. Paul does not argue in a negative way, contrasting the Greek world with Christ, or confusing the two. On the contrary, he treats the unknown God as a possible starting-point for his preaching of Christ's death and resurrection. The second point is the revelation granted to Israel, and the culminating point, after the Greek unknown God and the God who revealed himself to Israel, is Christ who died and rose again.

The method used by Paul in preaching to the Athenians was the one usually followed by missionaries in the countries in which Biblical revelation was unknown. The Congolese *Nzambi Mpungu* (the Supreme or Almighty God) was the point of contact between the Congolese religious world and Biblical revelation. This point of contact is not established once for all, but must rather be continually re-established between our own religious, social, economic, political, artistic and cultural world on the one hand, and Christ Himself on the other hand.

In contact with the word of God, and in the presence of the Holy Spirit, we are continually called both to leave our world behind, and to take it with us, so that Christ may become more and more our Saviour and Lord.

4

SACRIFICE

S O MUCH MATERIAL is already available on the question of Sacrifice that it is imperative that we should seek primarily to clear the ground in terms of the African environment. But more important still is the fact that in almost every territory in this vast continent sacrifices are offered daily either for the preservation of health; for the appeasement of some vengeful spirits; for the celebration of a deity; or for the appeasement or the glorification of the ancestral spirits. At sowing- or at harvest-time; in times of peril or drought; at the birth of a child, or the death of an aged adult, a whole range of rites is performed which require the offer of some sacrifice. This may be in the form of grain or an egg or an animal, and, in the ultimate case, of a human being. That this factor in the life of the African has not been given much, if any, attention by Christian evangelists for over a century in most parts of Africa is a matter of much regret.

My own interpretation of this neglect has so far been that the majority of Christian missions operating in West Africa are of the Reformed Churches, although one yet has to discover why the Roman Catholic missions, who obviously understand the concept of Sacrifice and observe it in the Sacrifice of the Mass, do not seem to have made any appreciable inroads into the practice of offering sacrifices by the Africans. It is quite surprising that Fr. Placide Tempels, writing of the Congo, has said very little of the factor of Sacrifice, although he is most illuminating on the concept of Power, *muntu,* and the role of that concept in the thought-forms of the people whom he discusses. Karl Laman's monographs on the Kongo are full of rites which imply sacrifices, but little attention is indeed given to these rites in a Sacrificial context. Even Canon J. V. Taylor,

57

who has demonstrated a closer understanding of the African religious situation than most, fails to understand this problem as the open sesame of the heart of the African to Christian teaching because of his own aversion to the doctrine of the Real Presence of Christ at the Eucharist.[1]

At a meeting of theological teachers in West Africa here at Ibadan in 1958, a reference to priestcraft and the role of the priest and the sacrificial factors in West Africa was heard with much resistance. This was all the more a pity, happening as it did in a discussion that followed an interesting talk by Bishop D. O. Awosika, then Assistant Bishop of Ondo. Only a few of the African members of the Conference saw the significance. The opposition was strongest from the European missionaries present, warmly supported by a number of their loyal African colleagues. Today, we are on the threshold of a new era when as Africans I hope we shall patiently seek to examine this subject and to discuss it openly without the inhibition of some European or other who feels obliged to eschew all mention of the subject and its significance to the Christian Church in Africa, because of an erstwhile revulsion that developed in Europe about four hundred years ago, and has since filtered across the Atlantic to the United States of America.

I propose in this paper first to illustrate various forms of Sacrifice offered in West Africa in particular, from which I hope to draw some specific inferences which would lead to one or two general considerations relating to the problem of Christian evangelism in Africa.

I. SOME INSTANCES OF SACRIFICES OFFERED

For over forty years, along one of the streets of Freetown, at two points, the one where four roads meet, and the other a T-junction with a side street, there have appeared, with unbroken regularity, sacrificial offerings left behind every day by some person or persons of course unknown to the public. Sometimes one sees a green pawpaw fruit cut into two, the halves laid open; at other times one sees grains of cleaned rice mixed with various other substances, including chillies, and a

---

[1] Fr. Placide Tempels, *Bantu Philosophy* (Paris, Présence Africaine, 1959); Karl V. Laman, *The Kongo*, 3 vols, London, Kegan Paul, 1953 ff.; J. V. Taylor, *The Primal Vision*, London, S.C.M. Press, 1963, see especially p. 200.

few coins thrown in. Early in November, 1965, I noticed a small mat rolled into a bundle with both ends tied up. The contents of the bundle were of course not visible to passers-by. But the fact that a sacrifice is offered at one or sometimes both of these road junctions every night is quite significant. In the last seventeen years I have passed along this street every day except for about eight weeks in the year, and my early impressions have been abundantly confirmed.

Enquiry into the purpose of such sacrifices has led me to conclude that they are intended to avert sickness, or to promote recovery from an illness, or to avert failure in business, or some other form of ill-fortune attributed to the influence of some evil spirit, but more often to witchcraft. In some cases the sacrifice is said to be offered to enhance success. The bundle of mat is said to be associated with sickness and death. Corpses are often buried in mats so tied. I have never been able to see any actual performances; but one night, travelling by car up to the College on Mount Aureol, after the midnight hour, my wife and I encountered a woman performing strange antics in the middle of the road just above a second crossroad. She dashed into the tall grass to avoid detection, but we identified her before she vanished. She was a regular professing Christian. No doubt there would be many others who offer the sacrifices in question and who are not Christian. But this one definite evidence, solitary though it may seem, indicates an aspect of the problem of Sacrifice which we shall have to mention later.

In the hinterland of Sierra Leone sacrificial rites abound. Thus, among the Mende of Sierra Leone, when a farmer decides to cultivate rice on a plot of ground, on arriving at the farm and before commencing to clear it, he first offers a sacrifice to the spirits of those who had previously farmed the plot. He then proceeds to prepare the soil; but before he sows the seed, he offers some seed-rice to the same spirits. Then, when the harvest is due, he offers the first-fruits of the crop, which are ground into a flour, to the spirits. Finally, at the end of the harvest, he makes a large feast as a sacrifice to round off the exercise.

In another case, a man who seeks fame may offer something precious which he later carries on his person. The object to whom the offering is made is never made clear. But the contrary case is known of ritual enacted to avert ill-luck or misfortune. A box full of stones is placed on the head of the person involved, the relatives lay their hands on the box and ask that the misfortune should be transferred to the box of stones. This is later kept close to the offerer's home or taken to a crossroad and deposited there. Here again there is no indication at all as to whom the offering is made. But it is not unlikely that ill-luck has been personalized into a spiritual agency which, it is supposed, tends to inhabit stones, and that the purpose of the ritual is to invoke the presence of the ill-disposed spirit which would then naturally enter into the box of stones and remain imprisoned in it. The Azazel goat of the Hebrew atonement ritual seems to fulfil a similar purpose.[2]

A similar but perhaps even more complex ritual is that performed by various groups in Sierra Leone when a child, for example, who has fallen ill, is said by a diviner to have been attacked by witches who are said to have eaten up its intestines or some other visceral organ. The diviner, or often a healing medicine-man, when asked to provide a cure, would ask for time during which he claims to be able to make contact with the witches and bargain for an exchange victim. This may turn out to be a chicken—a red cock or a white hen, or sometimes even a sheep. The victim is then offered in sacrifice, the mother and usually the child himself and other relatives being present and laying hands on the victim. (The mother would hold the hand of the child if it was an infant.) The victim so offered is then regarded as having been given in exchange for the child. The difficulty, however, arises when one recalls that the witches are said to assume a spirit form, viz. that of the personality-soul—and attack the personality-soul of their victim.[3]

When, therefore, the sacrifice is offered, it is natural to conclude that the personality-soul of the victim is offered to the personality-souls of the attacking witches.[4] The Mende define

---

[2] For a good discussion of the Sacrifice of the goat to Azazel, see G. B. Gray, *Sacrifice in the Old Testament*, Oxford, Clarendon Press, 1925, pp. 316 ff. John Middleton tells of a scapegoat which the Lugbara send to the mountains in cases of an epidemic of meningitis or of drought (*Lugbara Religion*, London, O.U.P., 1960, pp. 114 f.).

[3] H. Debrunner, *Witchcraft in Ghana*, Kumasi, Presbyterian Book Depot, 1959, cap. 4, *imp* p. 19 ff.

[4] *Ibidem*, p. 89.

the object of this rite by saying that sometimes a particular individual would have been suspected of witchcraft, and therefore of being responsible for the child's illness. In which case the offering is made to him.

The Yoruba *Ebọ Etutu*. This is a severe sacrifice offered at nights, often after the people living in the neighbourhood had been warned to stay indoors while the rite is performed. In modern times, when the sacrifice is offered with regard to an illness, a sheep is killed and the carcase is treated with oil. It is then taken out of the house and may be laid at the foot of an *iroko* tree. If it is specifically a substitutionary sacrifice, the sheep is treated as a corpse and buried. It is believed that the sacrifice is offered to appease a wrathful spirit responsible for the illness. What is significant is the further belief that the first person to pass by that *iroko* tree the next day will attract the illness of the patient to himself. Idowu calls this rite a "Sacrifice of appeasement".[5] But it is difficult to associate appeasement with the probable suffering of an otherwise healthy person who goes out early on an honest business. In the old days human sacrifice was offered at this rite, especially so when the whole community was involved.

But perhaps most popular of all sacrifices are those offered to the ancestors. Rattray tells us that "The older Ashanti men and women never partake of food or drink without putting a morsel of the one and a few drops of the other in the ground for the *samanfo*" (i.e. the spirits of the departed).[6] The offering of food and libations to the dead is so commonplace that one need not enter into any lengthy description of its significance. The great Adae and Odwera ceremonies of Ghana are all without exception essentially instances of sacrificial rites performed to invoke the help of the ancestors. The descriptions which may be found in Rattray's *Ashanti* or in Busia's *The Position of the Chief in the Modern Political System of Ashanti* make it unnecessary for any detailed accounts to be given here. It is significant that in Ghana there has been a pro-

[5] E. B. Idowu, *Olodumare*, London, Longmans, 1962, p. 123. A large tree is usually associated with spirits; cp. R. S. Rattray, *Ashanti*, London, O.U.P., 1923, pp. 258 ff.; some other instances are as follows: in Guinea, Sierra Leone and Western Nigeria, the cotton tree; in Western Nigeria the *iroko* and in Northern Nigeria, the *baobab* tree.

[6] R. S. Rattray, *op. cit.*, p. 137; cp. pp. 215, n. 3, 216.

liferation of pagan shrines after World War II.[7] These shrines work on a system of sacrifices offered at an altar which may be seen by a vistor privileged to enter the precincts. They also operate on a system of possessions which affect the priest or priestess who can then prescribe cures for illness and adjudicate when a theft or witchcraft has been committed. Thus, at the Mframaso shrine, for example, suppliants are often asked to take a chicken to the deity. If such a chicken is placed on the *Nyame dua* and it pecks the paste of eggs previously smashed on it, "the deity has accepted the sacrifice and will help the suppliant. The *okyeame* (i.e. the spokesman) then wrings off the bird's head and drops the blood on the *dua*", and other objects used by the priest. The decapitated chicken is then thrown into the yard and left to be consumed by vultures, except in cases where it happens to be large, when "small boys forestall the vultures and gleefully run off with it for supper".[8]

We cannot exhaust the types of sacrifices generally offered. But the aforementioned instances give a brief conspectus of the type which one may come across in various parts of West Africa.

We shall therefore go on to discuss the structure and purpose of the African sacrificial rites in general, in the hope of discovering a pattern or patterns.

II. THE STRUCTURE AND PURPOSE OF THE SACRIFICIAL RITES IN AFRICA

Basically, the sacrifices are offered to a spirit, however indefinite, who is supposed to be more powerful than human beings in the natural state, sometimes to the ancestors who, now spirits, are more powerful than the living, and in a few rare instances to the Supreme God. Rattray tells of "beautifully designed temples of the Sky God", hidden away "in remote corners of the older palaces".[9] At the same time, *Nyame* has no public temples although in every compound the *Nyame dua*, a tripodal altar, holds a basin or a pot into which are

---

[7] See M. J. Field, *Search for Security*, London, Faber, 1960, Pt. 1, Cap. 4. See Barbara Ward in *Africa*, Vol. X, 1937, p. 308; K. A. Busia, *op. cit.*, London, O.U.P., 1951, pp. 27 ff.

[8] Margaret Field, *op. cit.*, p. 126; cp. H. Debrunner, *op. cit.*, p. 126. Debrunner also mentions the use of a sacrifice of a chicken after a victim's confessions of witchcraft.

[9] Rattray, *op. cit.*, p. 142.

placed offerings made to *Nyame*. Though J. B. Danquah comments that "Akan religion, in its highest expression is the worship of the race",[10] yet he observes that *Nyankopon* may be addressed in salutations and prayers and worshipped as *Amen*.[11] He is the Father God of the Akan.[12] The other national groups said to worship God are chiefly the Kaffirs, the Kposso, the Ewe and the Kikuyu.[13] The Kikuyu situation is unique in some respects. No regular prayers or other religious ceremonies are organized for the Supreme God *Ngai*, but at the major crises of life—birth, initiation, marriage and death—communication may be held with *Ngai*. When the people are happy they must not pester *Ngai* with prayers and thanksgivings. But when he punishes someone for, say, looking up towards the sky during a thunderstorm when lightning flashes around, or on serious occasions like drought or an outbreak of an epidemic or a severe illness, a sacrifice may be offered to *Ngai*![14] Prayers for rain come under this category. Among the Mende of Sierra Leone, for example, it is usual to call upon God in a crisis but only in a short ejaculatory statement. One must hurry. But no sacrifices are offered to Him. There are however, instances of sacrifice being offered to the supreme God among the Yoruba and Igbo.[15] We may therefore say that sacrifices offered directly to the Supreme God are rare, and even where instances of this are found there are no priests who serve Him at a regular altar.[16]

On the other hand, everywhere there are temples, or altars erected to the worship of the cultic spirits. The practice varies

[10] J. B. Danquah, *The Akan Doctrine of God*, London, Lutterworth Press, 1944, p. 169; cp. Section 4, Cap. III.

[11] *Ibid.*, p. 47; cp. J. V. Taylor, *op. cit.*, p. 87; *Présence Africaine*, July, 1958, p. 87.

[12] J. B. Danquah, *ibid.*, Section 1, Cap. III.

[13] Eva Meyerowitz, *The Akan of Ghana*, London, Faber, 1958, p. 83 f.

[14] Jomo Kenyatta, *Facing Mount Kenya*, London, Mercury Books, 1961, Cap. X; cp. Mircea Eliade, *The Myth of the Eternal Return*, London, Routledge & Kegan Paul, 1955, p. 96 ff.; *Patterns in Comparative Religion*, London and New York, Sheed & Ward, 1958, pp. 47–57.

[15] See E. B. Idowu, *op. cit.*, Cap. II; J. O. Lucas, *The Religion of the Yorubas*, Lagos, 1948, p. 44 ff.

[16] Dr. Idowu describes a simple ritual directed to *Olodumare* at which the worshipper first makes a circle of chalk or ashes, pours a libation of cold water and places a kola-nut on cotton wool in the centre of the circle. He then breaks up the kola-nut and offers a prayer to *Olodumare* with the kola-nut held between his outstretched hands towards the sky. (*Ibid.* p. 142.)

63

in the case of the ancestral spirits. In Sierra Leone, for example, one often comes across a small hut not far from a river which forms a worshipping centre for the celebration of the founding fathers who had died in war by the riverside entrance to the town or village. In this house is usually kept a mushroom-shaped black ant-hill (Mende, *kɔkɔi*), representing the circular mud huts with conical thatched roofs together with a succulent plant (*costus afer*, Mende, *hɔwɛi*) suggestive of the continued existence of the ancestors. At the entrance of the hut a large stone is set on which the priest sits to perform the necessary rites. At graveside ceremonies food is set by the head of the grave, thus providing a crude primitive form of altar. In some cases there are regular priests associated with the rites, but often the oldest member of the family makes the petitions and offers the sacrifices. The role of the nature-divinities is of course complex and so there is no clear pattern of the worship, but some of the cultic centres have their priests and altars. In general the mode of worship of the nature-divinities is of the same *genre* as that of the ancestors. Most of the priests of the new shrines in Ghana claim to have received a revelation from some spirit after an ecstatic experience which takes them into the forest.[17] In view of the wide usage of sacrifices and the variety of sacrificial rites that exist, any understanding of the *raison d'être* of the rites requires some classification. This we shall now undertake under two heads.

(a) *With reference to the object to whom the sacrifice is offered*

Six main classes may be isolated:

(*a*) Sacrifices to vengeful spirits, associated with disaster and illnesses, or even death.

(*b*) Sacrifices to those who practise that form of witchcraft which is based on a replica of the personality-soul.

(*c*) Sacrifices offered to the ancestors.

[17] Cp. M. J. Field, *op. cit.*, Part I, Cap. III; cp. Eva Meyerowitz, *The Sacred State of the Akan*, London, Faber, 1961, p. 123 f. for an account of the revelation of the God later known as *Tano Kwado Twumpuduro*; Busia also gives two accounts of similar experiences, the one of *Di Amono* of Gyansoso, near Wenchi, and the other of *Kwaku Fri*. (See Daryll Forde, *African Worlds*, London, O.U.P. 1955, p. 193 f.)

(d) Sacrifices offered to a wide range of vague, indeterminate spirits better described as personalized agencies, e.g. the sacrifice for fame.

(e) Sacrifices offered to defined nature-divinities associated with trees, rivers, rocks and like objects.

(f) Sacrifices implying the presence of a spirit, representing the psychic powers of the participants—a projected spirit.

These classes are neither exclusive nor are they exhaustive. The first five classes are easily recognized, so we shall here only comment on the sixth class. The spirit implied is not at all objective. Indeed, none is mentioned. But when, as in Sierra Leone in the pre-Independence days, a paramount chief called together the tribal authorities to a rendezvous and asked them to promise never to betray his actions to the British Government, they took an oath on a pumpkin, each member of the group laying his hands on the fruit. Later the fruit was shot through with a gun and cut up into a number of pieces equal to that of the participants, which they then took home to cook and eat, thus testifying to their continued adherence to the vow. The act of shooting through the fruit symbolized the fate of anyone who recanted later on. The consumption of the cooked portions by the participants sealed their identification each with the other and with the whole group. Eating a portion of the pumpkin symbolized that each member had taken into himself both himself and all his colleagues. In effect this was an oath-taking ceremony, but we suggest that the rite was also sacrificial.

In this connection we must mention the blood covenant—another oath-taking ceremony. Briefly, this rite in its simple form is performed by two persons, say X and Y, and amounts to X cutting his arm and drawing blood from it, which he wipes off with something edible—e.g. a kola-nut in Nigeria or a coffee-berry in East Africa. Y does the same. Both parties then swop kola-nuts and eat the exchanged nut. From that time on the two parties regard themselves in a bond of brotherhood stronger than that between intra-uterine brothers. So they nevermore deceive, nor do they betray each other. In Nigeria, business men often enter into a blood-covenant with their factors, before giving them any wares for sale, especially if the latter have to travel to distant places. Any default, it is believed, is attended by death. The fundamental nature of the act is the offer in sacrifice of one's blood to another which he eats. Sometimes the rite is quite elaborate, as in the cases of Lord Lugard's otherwise futile and empty pacts with the chiefs of various East African tribes.[18] One is, however, compelled to accept that the parties concerned believe that from the moment of making the contract some spirit has been brought into being which remains ever watchful for any defection. If ever the pact is broken, this spirit descends with a vengeance and destroys the defaulter.

In this context we wish to put forward the suggestion that circumcision constitutes a sacrifice, particularly so when it forms a constituent factor in the African puberty rites. We will not here go into the origins of circumcision. But the classic case of Zipporah's offer of the foreskin of her son Gershom by touching the feet of Moses with it (Ex. 4: 25) seems to be an offer of a sacrifice. A. J. Reinach suggests that boys are made to seal a covenant with the deity of the clan by the offer of the blood of manhood. He therefore posits that this was the case with Gershom, whose blood vicariously sealed a covenant with Yahweh.[19]

In the West African situation, Camara Laye's description of the rite is certainly suggestive of a sacrifice. An all-night dancing ceremony when the boys are not allowed to sleep, after a

[18] M. Perham and Mary Bull, *The Diaries of Lord Lugard*, 3 vols., London, Faber, 1959, Vol. I, pp. 301, 416.

[19] Cp. *Revue des Etudes Ethnographiques et Sociologiques*, Paris, 1908. Article by A. J. Reinach on *La Lutte de Yahvé avec Jacob et avec Moïse et l'origine de la circoncision*.

B. S. Childs, *Myth and Reality in the Old Testament*, 2nd edition, London, S.C.M. Press, 1962, pp. 59–65.

Canon Lindsay Dewar in *Journal of Theological Studies*, New Series, Vols. 3–4, 1952–53, pp. 205–208. Article, "Biblical Use of the Term Blood".

We would here draw attention to the fact that B. S. Childs also suggests that the story describes an act by which Zipporah provided vicarious circumcision for Moses thus appeasing the sinister local demon who by chance inhabited the particular place where Moses and his family were spending the night. Canon Lindsay Dewar, without going into the question of the deity concerned, says that the story describes the potency of blood in the rite of circumcision. He also observes that in some of those rites, "The blood of circumcision is allowed to fall on to other members of the tribe, thereby signifying the union thus believed to be cemented between the initiate and the rest of the tribe."

series of frightening experiences, creates a feeling of anxiety designed, it seems, to lead the initiates to the great moment when one feels fear but either is too afraid to shout for help or indeed ceases to bother about the fearful sight any more. When the rite is performed, Camara Laye records the head of the cult (*sema*) as saying, "the blood must flow ... If it did not flow ...", a sentence never completed.[20] Colin Turnbull, commenting on the rite as performed in Ndola, describes how Ibrahim, one of his characters, regretted that he had been circumcised in a hospital and had not been allowed to go through the tribal demands of facing the rite in cold blood and "sharing blood" with his brothers.[21] Camara Laye says that at a stage in the preliminary proceedings, when apparently the desire to attain manhood had been aroused in him, he and his co-initiates had become prepared to pay for the privilege of entering into "man's estate" "with their blood".[22] Eliade suggests that in some parts of Africa circumcision means death; the act of circumcision symbolizing the destruction of the genitals, an act which shows that the intention is to kill. Unfortunately, he does not develop this statement.[23] In Liberia, where the puberty rites alternate annually between the boys and the girls, the prepuce is said to be preserved for a ritual meal by the girls when they are initiated. The process is repeated, in reverse, when the girls are initiated.[24]

It is strongly believed that, among the Mende of Sierra Leone, a portion of the clipping of the clitoris which is removed when the girls are initiated into Sande is preserved and later eaten ritually at a special meal before the candidates graduate, at the ceremony called *nda hiti* or *kpɔyɔ wɛlɛ gbei*. Laubscher,

[20] Camara Laye, *The African Child*, London, Fontana Books, 1954, p. 104. For an account of the earlier experiences see pp. 82 ff.

[21] Colin Turnbull, *The Lonely African*, London, Chatto & Windus, 1963, Chapters 4, 9.

[22] Camara Laye, *op. cit.*, p. 94.

[23] M. Eliade, *Birth and Re-birth*, New York, Harper, 1958, p. 23.

[24] Cp. G. W. Harley, *Notes on the Poro in Liberia*, Papers of the Peabody Museum of American Archaeology and Ethnology, Harvard University, Vol. XIX, No. 2, 1941, p. 15. Bruno Bettelheim, *Symbolic Wounds*, London, Thames & Hudson 1955, p. 159 f. Bettelheim notes that in Western Australia the foreskin of a novice who has been circumcised is presented to his sister, who dries it, smears it with white ochre and wears it suspended from her neck. Among some of the other tribes the blood of the wound is collected in a shield and taken to the mother of the initiate, who drinks some of it and gives food to the man who brought it.

referring to the initiation rites of the Fingu and Tembu tribes in the South-Eastern Cape of South Africa, which rites include circumcision, states that "the actual surgical mutilation, or circumcision, apart from being a test of fitness for manhood and initiation into manhood, must also be considered as a form of sacrifice". He goes on: "It is a sacrifice or atonement in retrospect and prospect. The boy is not giving up a part of his sexual organ for forbidden acts already committed, but because there is some guilt about his attachment to his mother in mind. The sacrifice is therefore a means of compromising with the conscience. The horror and disgust with which the pagans view sexual intercourse between a wife and an uncircumcised lad show the incestuous meaning that is read in such an act where the prepuce is still intact, because the word wife denotes the mother class."[25]

Our own view is that the rite of circumcision gives the patient an opportunity of dropping some of his blood on the ground which is in most African circles supposed to be the origin of life and of the child. It is also the abode of the dead. So at circumcision, the parents encourage the lad to give up some of his life back to the source from which it is derived, viz. the Earth and the ancestral spirits who are often thought to have re-entered the new-born babe. Thus the youth enters into a covenant which qualifies him to be taught certain moral codes and the history and traditions of the land.[26]

(b) *With reference to the offerings*

We may identify four main types:

(a) Goodwill offerings of blood, food and drink as in cases of celebrating the death of a relative, or commemorating the death of an ancestor, or invoking the support of the ancestors for some undertaking to be embarked upon by a member of the family.

Under this class come libations. In the Western Area of Sierra

---

[25] B. J. F. Laubscher, *Sex, Custom and Psychopathology*, London, Routledge & Kegan Paul, 1951 (reprint), p. 136.

[26] It should be mentioned here that the blood that flows after clitoridectomy seems to be prevented from reaching the Earth. The Kikuyu, for example, spread a skin on the ground on which the initiates sit (cp. Jomo Kenyatta, *op. cit.*, p. 145).

Leone, for example, many Christians at the great Festivals of the Church, but chiefly at Christmas and Easter, visit the graves of their dead and offer water and alcoholic spirits to make their hearts cool whilst either pouring their hearts' complaint or invoking their aid for the future. At ceremonies associated with the ancestors, chickens are killed early in the morning and the blood allowed to flow into a hole specially dug for that purpose. Some of the cooked food is also offered in the evening at the same hole. Sometimes two holes are dug. The libations poured even at airports are similar in character.

(b) Propitiatory or appeasement offerings of an animal, as in the case of the Yoruba *Ebo Etutu*, or exchange victims to witches.

Here too the blood of the victim, as well as the meat, also laden with blood, constitute the offering.

(c) Mediatory offerings of food and drink. In the old days human sacrifice was prominent in this type of offering.

Cases of these are known, for example, among the Mende of Sierra Leone when the ancestors are requested to first accept an offering and then to pass it on to a tree or river-spirit. In the days of domestic slavery, a slave was usually killed and his blood allowed to flow on to the ground for the benefit of the ancestors.

(d) Integrative offerings, chiefly of blood.

These belong primarily to the group of rites like those which establish a blood covenant between two persons, and circumcision as we have described it.[27] At the same time, the feasts associated with the ancestors always include a peace-making factor by which any disputes between members of the extended family are settled and misunderstandings resolved.

We may now go on to say that the sacrifices we have mentioned are associated with cleanness and uncleanness; guilt and sickness; peace, coolness of heart and reconciliation; absolution and the restoration of health; concern for the well-

---

[27] The case of an elder woman in Ghana who, after bringing forth an *obosom*, sacrifices her eldest daughter at the foot of the *gya dua kra*, planted at the entrance of the township of her new clan, is of this order. See Eva Meyerowitz, *op. cit.*, p. 27.

being of the dead by the living and active help and support for the living by the dead; group fellow-feeling, sometimes between members of a tribe, but most times between members of a family or a clan or between a group of two or more bound together by a common purpose; disruption and restoration. Whilst therefore we may readily accept that a deity or a cultic spirit, or some ancestral spirit or spirits, are usually the objects of the sacrifices, there is much evidence to suggest that the rites have a societary aspect. Such evidence is seen clearest in the case of the prophylactic sacrifices, which are offered in cases of illness. Thus, among the Mende of Sierra Leone, for example, violations of the incest taboos lead to stomach pains and sleepiness for the adults and a pot-belly condition for a child, where the woman has one. When a man, say, notices he suffers from these conditions, he or his relatives and friends consult a diviner, who then diagnoses that the patient has violated the *Humɔi* cult. The patient therefore goes to the priest of the cult to seek medical aid. He is then asked to sit down and spun thread is webbed around his great toes, his thumbs and ears, and he confesses the whole truth; a chicken is then killed as a sacrifice and its blood sprayed on the patient to absolve him. He is then sprayed with a medication consisting of leaves crushed in water; sometimes this is followed by an exorcising of the evil symbolized by the illness; he then takes a ritual bath, which is followed by a communal meal by all present, after some of the food consisting of the sacrificial chicken and rice has been first offered to the *Humɔi* spirit. In some cases the patient and his immediate relatives are publicly castigated.[28]

The mechanics of this rite seem to suggest that the offence is one of which society disapproves, and anyone who is guilty of it is essentially ostracized from society. Tribal society is, however, a closed society. So public opinion drives an offender on to seek restoration into society without intermission and without mercy. At the same time, a cultic spirit is introduced to give authority to the weight of public opinion. The guilty party must therefore appease the cultic spirit. However, the forgiveness offered by the cultic priest does not exonerate the

---

[28] Among the Kono, a neighbouring tribe, those so castigated have to go about naked and are flogged along the entire length of the village; cp. R. T. Parsons, *Religion in an African Society*, Leiden, Brill, 1964, pp. 34 f.

offender from the societal disapproval of his behaviour. He must also be punished. So, as stated, in one form of *Humɔi* he is publicly flogged, together with his brothers and sisters. In another type of *Humɔi*, which does not employ the whip, the offenders are required to take a ritual bath around the cultic stone which is at the entrance of the village or town, and women, who are invariably protected from close male view when they are bathing, must do so in public with men standing around. The women, in particular, because of their offence, lose the dignity which society accords them until they have completed the rites, when society restores them into its fold and they are fully forgiven. Ritual nudity becomes the means of restoring the integrity and plenitude, more so, of the women.[29] This reaction of society is integrally related to the fact that the whole process of moral education of the Mende, in this instance on sex-relations, produces in them a built-in mechanism which causes the illness. That is to say that their conscience disapproves of their action and they fall ill. Hence, when the cultic rites have been performed and the offenders know they have paid the penalty of their actions, they go home either feeling well or feeling optimistic of early recovery. We have no statistics of such recoveries, but our analysis of the situation suggests that the cultic spirit is fundamentally a medium by which society exacts punishments of those who violate its moral codes.[30]

We may therefore go on to say that the appeasement factor in the sacrifice is in fact inherent in the rite more so than the suggestion that it is directed towards a deity or a cultic spirit. This inherent quality referred to in this context is applicable to the other sacrifices. Joyful, covenantal and mediatorial rites are all equally what they are because they are associated with social situations which call for those responses. The blood-covenants are most significant here, as indeed there is no god as such who is invoked by the participants. When a god or some cultic spirit or the ancestral spirits are postulated, the sacrifice enhances the authority. The subject who submits himself to

[29] Cp. M. Eliade, *Images and Symbols*, London, Harvill Press, 1963, p. 158.
[30] Cp. Leonard Hodgson, *The Doctrine of the Atonement*, London, Nisbet, 1951, p. 61. His discussion on punishment and forgiveness is easily applicable in this context, if instead of God we read the cultic spirit.

being tied around with spun thread, to meeting the demands of confession, to accepting absolution, whether with blood or with a medicated fluid or both, to taking a bath in public view and, sometimes, to suffering public castigation, does so only if he accepts that the deity or spirit is in control of his life and behaviour, and exercises its authority through the enactment of certain specific codes of behaviour and taboos.[31] To comply with these is to be ritually clean and to violate them is to be unclean. Ritual cleanliness accordingly is indicated by being an approved member of society. To be unclean is intrinsically to be outside the pale of society. This is barrenness.

These attitudes are based on the fact that "To primitive man life is Power, not Law".[32] This Power is principally a Fertility Power. So goodness is power; health and strength represent Power at work. Evil is therefore a contrary, foreign and hostile power which detracts from the natural Power with which man is endowed. The fount of all Power is, of course, God. God is therefore a great *Muntu*. Man, himself a *muntu*, comes second in the Power hierarchy and is naturally able to induce Power into other objects, animate and inanimate, whilst he is himself prone to destruction at the hand of an adverse power.[33] Since the balance is restored through offerings of sacrifices, these therefore seem to be media which enhance the Power of man or of the spirts, ancestral or cultic. It is in this context that one can appreciate why medicine-men wield so much power in Africa, and why priestly functions at sacrifices provide the strongest influences to maintain the unity of the community after a breach of societary regulations. Thus, in Eastern Nigeria, the priest of *Ala*, the Earth-Goddess, is usually a head-chief, and among the Yoruba the Ifa priests have been the centre of the most vital influences which have moulded the life of the people.[34]

In a short paper one cannot exhaust the problems associated

---

[31] Cp. *Harvard Theological Review*, Vol. XLIV, No. 3, July, 1947, H. J. Rose on *Numen* and *Mana*.

[32] G. van der Leeuw, *Religion in Essence and Manifestation*, New York and Evanston, Harper Torchbook edition, 1963, vol. I, p. 56, chs. 1-4.

[33] Cp. Fr. Placide Tempels, *op. cit.*, pp. 30-37, 64-70, 78. The whole book is most useful on this point.

[34] Cp. P. Amaury Talbot, *Some Nigerian Fertility Cults*, London, O.U.P., 1927, p. 12; E. B. Idowu, *op. cit.*, passim; Fela Sowande, *Ifa*, Lagos, 1964.

with sacrifice as we know it in West Africa. But let us now briefly examine three aspects.

(1) *Its Origin*

From what has been said so far, we can more definitely say how sacrifices are operated and to what end, but no one seems able to be certain as to how they came to be instituted.

We recall that Yerkes has pointed out that on big occasions when a group, either of members of a family or of a clan, found themselves in a situation when the sense of "human finiteness was more acute, as before going on a trek or striking camp, or before entering a battle or after the successful performance of these acts, or after failure", they met "together to share the power or the courage . . ." of some animal which they had come to feel was "greater than they", on the assumption that what "had been eaten passed into the eater. . . ."[35] This common sharing of the same power bound them into a kinship which transcended that of blood, and we would call this result *incorporation* resulting from *participation*. The participants develop a bond of fellowship and therefore of *esprit de corps* which provides mutual support each towards the other. This is in effect another aspect of the Power complex. It is certainly the basis of the force of the blood-covenant. But beyond this it is difficult to go. It is significant that even with regard to the organized cultus of Hebrew religion, Köhler could say, "There is no suggestion anywhere in the Old Testament that Sacrifice or any other part of the cult was instituted by God. It knows only the regulation of already existing sacrifice by divine institution."[36] Later, he says, "The cult was originally man's attempt to express to God his gratitude, his supplications, his confession, his desire to atone, his excuses, his worship."[37]

Even if Yerkes is right, following Robertson Smith and others, to stress the communion factor of Sacrifice as primary, we would however go on to say that embedded in communion is the

[35] R. K. Yerkes, *Sacrifice*, London, Black, 1953, p. 20 f.; see the whole of Chapter III.

[36] L. Köhler, *Old Testament Theology*, London, Lutterworth Press, 1957, p. 181 f. Masure interestingly observes that man invented sacrifices. See *The Christian Sacrifice*, London, Burns & Oates, 1947, p. 71.

[37] *Ibid.*, p. 197.

sense of mutual give and take. In other words, the sacrifice assumes a gift factor also.[38]

In West Africa in particular, it seems as if all sacrifice is a gift, a gift of homage, which sometimes, but by no means always, takes the form of a meal.[39] Indeed, the general association of libations with almost every rite in West Africa suggests that this gift aspect of the sacrifices offered is paramount.[40] When one studies the prayers offered at the sacrifices they are generally petitionary in character.[41] The nature of the petitions and intercessions do not support the view that the gifts are bribes— to the gods as well as to the ancestral spirits. Thus Gundry, for example, rejects out of hand the gift theory of sacrifice and prefers "some elementary *rationale* of sacrifice, even if the worshipper is not always conscious of it". He concedes fellow-feeling as a motive for sacrifices to the dead but looks for another in the case of supernatural beings. He thus decides for bribery, which to him is "a gift to flatter a god and so buy his favour".[42] We, however, wonder whether the sacrificial

[38] Robertson Smith, of course, makes a sharp distinction between the communal meal and the gift form of sacrifice (*Religion of the Semites*, New Edition, London, Black, 1894, Lecture VII, XI, *imp.* pp. 244 f., 398).

[39] Cp. K. A. Busia, *The Position of the Chief in the Modern Political System of the Ashanti*, London, O.U.P., 1951, p. 31 f., where the author gives a good account of the *Odwera* Festival.

[40] J. H. Nketia, for instance, writes: "In Ghana, popular imagination has seized upon libation as a possible contribution which African worship can offer to the Christian Church. Libation is interpreted by many educated Christians as a concrete method of prayer which they consider ritually satisfying and helpful in the concentration of their faculties." (*The Church in Changing Africa*, Report of the All Africa Conference of Churches, Ibadan, A.A.C.C., 1955; pp. 64 f.)

[41] E. B. Idowu, *op. cit.*, p. 116; cp. Jomo Kenyatta, *op. cit.*, p. 239. A prayer recorded by Bishop Adjayi Crowther and the Rev. J. C. Taylor at Onitsha on March 5, 1859, to a god Tshi at a sacrifice (*guo moa*), gives antiquity to the statement. (A goat was killed and the blood allowed to run over the stumps of sticks placed in a bowl to present to the god.) The prayer ran: "I beseech thee my guide, make me good; thou hast life. I beseech thee to intercede God, the Spirit; tell Him my heart is clean. I beseech thee to deliver me from all bad thoughts in my heart; drive out all witchcraft; let riches come to me; see (i.e. here is) your sacrificial goat; see your kola-nuts; see your rum and palm-wine." *The Gospel on the Banks of the Niger*, London, Seeley Service 1859, Vol. 1, p. 348. Busia has a similar prayer offered at an *Odwera* Ceremony at Wenchi which reads: "Drobo, today the edges of the year have met. The Chief of Wenchi has given you yams, he has given you sheep, he has given you eggs, and now he has brought this drink. Let Wenchi prosper. May the women bear children; do not let our children die; those who have gone to trade, may they get money. May there be peace and prosperity during the present chief's reign" (*op. cit.*, p. 30).

[42] D. W. Gundry, *Religions*, London, Macmillan, 1958, p. 68.

gifts can be a bribe at all, that is, "a reward given to pervert the judgment or corrupt the conduct", according to the Shorter Oxford English Dictionary. We think not. It would, however, be fair to say that the offer of gifts always assumes a return present from the recipient. Jomo Kenyatta indeed makes it clear that the Kikuyu pray to their Supreme God, *Mwene-Nyaga,* and expect their prayers to be favourably answered "in return for the present given". He further states that the prayers to the ancestors are governed also by the law of "give and take".[43]

To maintain the gift theory, however, requires some consideration of the old phrase, *do ut des,* "I give that you may give". Space forbids a full discussion of this, but we would call attention to the fact that in the African situation it is bad form not to receive a gift and worse still not to give often a bigger gift in return. So the Mende of Sierra Leone who visits often takes with him a present, *fama lo (le),* a greeting kola-nut, which was originally in the form of a kola-nut, but today may be in a form of a chicken or some crop from his garden or farm. Not to receive this gift implies that the person is not really welcome. In return, the host must give his visitor some present when he leaves, usually one bigger than what he received. This is known as acknowledging the greeting, *fama gbual i.* The Sierra Leone Creole would complain bitterly if a visit is not acknowledged by the offer of even a cup of water: "*I nɔ gi mi wata sɛf*", they say. Among some of the tribes of Eastern Nigeria, as well as among the Yoruba, a visitor is always given a present of kola-nuts as an acknowledgment of his visit. Not to be given kola-nuts when one visits the Eastern Nigerians is to be told that one was not welcome. We would therefore adopt van der Leeuw's language and say that "To offer somebody something, ... is to offer someone a part of oneself; similarly, to accept a thing from another person is to receive some portion of his spiritual being, of his soul; and under these circumstances, the reciprocal nature of giving is quite obvious."[44]

[43] Jomo Kenyatta, *op. cit.,* p. 236.
[44] G. van der Leeuw, *op. cit.,* Vol. II, p. 351 f. Walter Eichrodt, referring to the primitive conception that everything by which a person influences his environment—his clothes, his weapons, hair-clippings, finger-nail parings—has the same living power as the whole personality of the individual, says that "In such a context a gift and the acceptance of a gift denote a real transference of power from one

(2) *The Use of Blood Rites*

Mention has already been made of the fact that there are various offerings made at sacrificial rites in West Africa—food crops of all kinds as well as animal victims. One would be inclined to generalize by saying that the food offerings have a strong fertility flavour, ranging from agricultural and human fertility to the removal of that which obstructs plenitude and success in one's undertakings. The animal victims are often used in cases of illnesses or for a variety of communal sacraments. As already pointed out, both forms are often combined at the communal occasions. But except in such rare cases as when the leg of a chicken is broken at the sacrifice and the chicken is let loose to wander about—the healing of the fracture being regarded as an index of the restoration of the health of the patient with a fractured leg—the animal victim is generally killed and eaten in whole or in part. When the animal is killed, its blood becomes a vital factor of the rite. Thus at an *Awujor* ceremony, among the Creole of Sierra Leone, the blood of the chickens offered is allowed to flow into the hole or holes dug for the Sacrifice at the first invocation of the ancestors, and the ancestors are invoked. Or again, at the Yoruba (*Ẹbọ Etutu*) rites, the carcase of the sheep may be treated with oil and laid at the foot of the *iroko* tree.

Circumcision, blood-covenant and human sacrifice are similar cases of the shedding of blood. As is well known to primitive man, blood represents life.[45] So the Akan do not practise circumcision, because it leads to the shedding of blood, which is life.[46] At the same time, menstruant blood is to them death radiating.[47] A Mende man must not attend a child-birth

---

system of personal life to another. . . ." (*Theology of the Old Testament*, Vol. 1, London S.C.M. Press, 1961, p. 155.) Cp. A. R. Johnson, *The Vitality of the Individual in the Thought of Ancient Israel*, Cardiff, U.P., 1949, p. 8. Van der Leeuw supports this point of view when he says, "The pivot of the Sacrificial act, its power centre, is always the gift itself: it must be given, that is to say, be set in motion. . . . It may be 'given' without any 'addressee' at all." He then adds: ". . . instead of the rationalistic *do ut des*, we must say, *do ut dares*, 'I give that thou mayest be able to give!'" (*op. cit*, p. 354).

[45] E. O. James, *op. cit.*, p. 146.

[46] Cp. Eva Meyerowitz, *op. cit.*, p. 31. The Gä, however, circumcise their boys up to the age of twelve. See M. J. Field, *Religion and Medicine of the Gä People*, London, O.U.P., 1961, p. 176.

[47] Cp. Eva Meyerowitz, *The Sacred State of the Akan*, London, Faber, 1951, p. 54.

because of the blood which accompanies the delivery. Meanwhile, it is universally accepted that blood, as life, represents the most precious gift one could offer. Blood symbolizes in its fullest extent the life of an individual.[48]

We may therefore isolate two distinct features of the blood-sacrifice: First, it creates a new bond among those who participate in the rite. This bond we earlier called "incorporation by participation". This aspect is seen at its clearest in the blood-covenant and in the instances we gave earlier of the age-mates who were circumcised at the same time. The blood shed at initiation ceremonies incorporates the initiate with the ancestors and the land of their birth. A similar explanation holds good for those who drink the blood sacrificed. Secondly, where a god is postulated, or where the ancestors are worshipped, it is believed that the blood revivifies the object to whom the offering is made. There is also the suggestion that it provides the fullest ground for bridging the gulf which has been caused by guilt.

Hence most blood-rites are both expiatory and propitiatory. At the same time, since blood is a gift, which is a vehicle of life offered to another, it not only revives the life of the recipients, but it also gives a new life to the donors. We are, however, faced with the use of blood to propitiate vengeful spirits, often unidentifiable. It will suffice to state here that since sacrificial blood is the most precious form of gift one could offer, therefore when the offerer identifies himself with the victim by laying on of hands, its blood, being life, more truly represents the life of the offerer than any other offering. The reciprocal gift to the offerer is accordingly of the highest order. He receives greater power than in the case of vegetable and other inanimate objects. It is in this context that we can understand why the elder woman, in Ghana, who, having become possessed of the *Kra* of *Nyame*, was expected to make the supreme sacrifice of a daughter at the age of puberty or a son, or one of her sisters or nieces, and to bury her under the *gya dua*

---

[48] On the question of blood offered representing the life and not the death of the victim, cp. Yerkes, *op. cit.*, Cap. V; W. Eichrodt, *op. cit.*, p. 163 n. 2; E. O. James, *op. cit.*, p. 146; Leon Morris, *The Apostolic Preaching of the Cross*, London, Tyndale Press, 1955, Chapter III. Article, "The Biblical Use of the term Blood", in *Journal of Theological Studies*, New Series, Vol. 3, October, 1952.

kra in order to ensure the well-being of the village to be.[49] A similar principle lies behind the slaying of a youth instead of the Akan King in order to ensure the revival of the king's *kra*.[50]

(3) *Is Sacrifice Expiation or Propitiation?*

Western theology has tended to distinguish these two terms, reserving the first for Christian thought and the latter essentially for pagan practices. The Christian God who is Love expiates sins but sinners propitiate an angry God. So C. H. Dodd would say that the use of the word propitiation in Romans 3: 25 "is . . . misleading, for it suggests the placating of an angry God", a sense foreign to biblical usage which stresses that "God alone could annul" sin.[51] Barrett is even more explicit when he says, "God cannot be said to propitiate man, still less his sin; he cleanses, and forgives, man and expiates (wipes out) his sin." But Barrett does state a caveat by adding the comment later on, that "it would be wrong to neglect the fact that expiation has, as it were, the effect of propitiation: the sin that might justly have excited God's wrath is expiated (at God's will), and therefore no longer does so."[52] Leenhardt, referring to the same verse says, "His (Jesus') Sacrifice takes the place of those sacrifices whose blood was sprinkled on the ark as a plea for pardon and an offering acceptable to Yahweh." But Leenhardt is working on the assumption that "Formerly God had instituted sacrificial rites with a gracious intention so as to manifest and effect His purpose of pardoning the guilt".[53] We are not discussing the text of the New Testament passage I have used. In any case it is difficult to determine the meaning behind St. Paul's use of the word *hilasterion*. Is it a place at which, or the means by which, God's forgiveness is given to man?[54] For our discussion, the interpretation of this word is an index of the basis of the attitude which has come to

[49] Eva Meyerowitz, *The Akan of Ghana*, p. 27. See note 31 above.
[50] Eva Meyerowitz, *The Divine Kingship in Ghana and Ancient Egypt*, London, Faber, 1960, p. 106.
[51] C. H. Dodd, *Romans*, London, Hodder & Stoughton 1932, p. 55.
[52] C. K. Barrett, *Romans*, London, Black, 1957, pp. 77f.
[53] F. J. Leenhardt, *Romans*, London, Lutterworth Press, 1961, pp. 102 f.; but see note 36 above.
[54] W. D. Davies, *Paul and Rabbinic Judaism*; London, S.P.C.K., 1948, pp. 230–242.

Africa, by which we think of an angry God whenever Sacrifice is mentioned.

Our description of various sacrificial rites in West Africa suggests that the angry-God-index is quite small. The sacrifices are generally to the gods and seldom to God. Mary Kingsley describes the African old gods as "The gods from whom he (the African) never expected pity, presided over by a god that does not care."[55] She was quite wrong. Certainly the ancestral spirits always showed pity and the Supreme God is always said to care even if not demonstrably. So the Mende man who has suffered grave injustice prays to God, saying "O God, see to it that you exercise your sovereignity." Indeed, any study of West African religious thought soon reveals that the fundamental offence against most cultic spirits is uncleanness. So sex intercourse between man and wife is not allowed before the Ghana shrine sessions or before participating in Yoruba worship.[56] In any case, sickness and sin and guilt are generally associated most of the time. The various taboos ensure sexual or some other form of social cleanness.[57] But, as we have seen, very few of the rites can be said to be appeasements of angry gods, because inherent in the cults is *Society* rather than a god. Ordinarily, the rites suggest joyous occasions as well as penitential ones; edification as well as rebuke. Even if some healing rites suggest appeasement, there are others which stress cleanness. The *Humɔi* rites of the Mende are in fact designed to remove that state of uncleanness characterized by a word *kaye*, translated, *rust*. Mende societary rules, without exception, lay great store by the moral obligations man owes to his fellow-man, some of which go with an offender beyond the grave. So, before a man is buried, all those whom he had offended come forward and state their grievance, and thus stay the concurrent curse. His debtors also state their claims and a representative of the family takes over the debt. The corpse, lying already by the side of the grave, is now ready to be buried. The spirit of the deceased is also now free from the stains of his guilt. If the test for witchcraft which follows proves

[55] Olwen Campbell, *Mary Kingsley*, London, Methuen 1957, p. 129.

[56] M. J. Field, *Search for Security*, p. 98; *Religion and Medicine of the Gã People*, p. 112. E. B. Idowu, *op. cit.*, p. 108.

[57] Cp. Eva Meyerowitz, *The Sacred State of the Akan*, p. 118; *The Akan of Ghana*, p. 31, and the references to *Humɔi* in the text.

negative, a layer of white sand is spread afterwards over the surface of the grave. But by far the widest range is covered by the descriptive word *rust*.

Hence, the concept of wiping stains, more so than that of placation, is predominant among the Mende.

In other words, the Christian theologian studying Sacrifice in West Africa has the task of finding out the areas in which placation occurs, and those in which *wiping out* a stain does occur in order to present the gospel in a way that can evoke a healthy meaning of the *hilasterion* concept to his audience.

Conclusion

A paper on Sacrifice must at least mention the problems of pluralism. If we would face up to the facts, it is absolutely certain that a large percentage of our compatriots find the use of pagan sacrifices a salve to their physical and mental troubles.[58] When I visited the Akonade Shrine in Ghana in December, 1962, I learnt with much interest that the priestess herself claimed to be a Christian and went to church from time to time. Reports which do not bear being reduced to print suggest that high-ranking leaders, as well as their humble followers of the working class, learned and ignorant, pagans and Christians, all find the problems of life weighing so heavily on them that they seek salvation through a recourse to pagan sacrifices. The Akonade Shrine has Christian clients. The popularity of the *Tigare* cult in Ghana is a case in point. Where then do we go from here? Busia watched an *Odwera* ceremony in Wenchi some time just before 1951 and, observing that Christians participated in the rites without any inhibition, questioned them as to how they felt. His account goes on to say, "Their answers were in many instances, 'I felt its reality' or 'I was deeply moved'."[59]

I have watched Sierra Leone Creole celebrating an *Awujɔ* feast. At the evening sacrifice, group after group were fully

[58] Cp. Onuora Nzekwu, *Blade Among the Boys*, London, Hutchinson, 1962, p. 139. This book presents, in a very graphic language, the all too easy belief in the potency of charms and the worship of the ancestors on the one hand, and the regular devotion to the practice of the Christian faith on the other, by Roman Catholics of Eastern Nigeria.

[59] K. A. Busia, *op. cit.*, p. 38.

involved in the rite. Not only did they come from far distances to share in the feast, but they allowed quarrels to be settled and misunderstandings to be resolved. At the *Nyɔlɛ*, they scrambled for the food that remained in the bowl with alacrity and without reserve.

Do we say with European Christians that this is all so much pagan nonsense that we must consign the participants to a hot hell? Or, should we in prayer ask for the wisdom of the Holy Spirit to discover what keeps our people so close to the sacrificial rites of pagan practice even when they have been brought up in Christian homes?[60] Orunmilaism is a Nigerian problem. The Ifa priests, when their cathedral at Ife is completed, will provide for the Yoruba a temple as substantial as any Christian seat of a Bishop. How is the Church in Nigeria going to meet that challenge? This is in fact a question for all of us. How shall we make our evangelism truly penetrative in Africa, particularly so in the days of a nationalistic recourse to the old gods?

Alioune Diop's comments at the First International Congress of Africanists in Accra, in December, 1962, is symptomatic of our problem: speaking about *Présence Africaine* he says, "Take religion, for instance, which is the most naturally serene of all, since more than any other it is the realm of meditation, contemplation and peace. It is astonishing for anyone who cares to reflect upon it, to note the flagrant contradictions, even crimes, which are committed quietly and unobtrusively in the sphere of religion. Since no African assumed the responsibility or took the initiative to intervene, religion in many instances actually fostered colonialism and neo-colonialism. To be more precise, because the authority of Western culture and Western institutions outstripped ours where the expression of faith was concerned, it succeeded in converting African Christians into a people without soul or visage, a pale shadow of the dominating pride of the Christian West. At the very heart and centre of the Church in Africa, we have in fact wit-

---

[60] Dr. J. O. Lucas observes that the "permanence" of Christianity among the Yoruba "cannot be guaranteed unless it is made 'a religion of heart and soul' " (*op. cit.*, p. 364). The late Bishop T. S. Johnson, Assistant Bishop of Sierra Leone, felt so strongly about this problem that he produced at his own expense a book, *Fear Fetish*, which was printed in Freetown in 1949.

nessed the mutilation of the African Personality, and the trampling of human dignity in Africa."[61]

Should Alioune Diop be left to say the last word on Christianity in Africa?

[61] *Proceedings of the First International Congress of Africanists, Accra, 11th–18th December, 1962,* London, O.U.P., 1964, pp. 50, 51.

5

THE THEOLOGICAL ESTIMATE OF MAN

The Theme

THE GENERAL THEME under which the subject of this paper has to be treated is "Biblical Revelation and African Beliefs". This immediately raises two difficulties. The first is that a theological estimate of man by its very nature is rooted in only one source, namely, the gospel from which it is a derivative. Hence, African beliefs cannot obviously be used as such. But the gospel addresses man—every man. It cannot possibly do so without taking into consideration man's estimate of himself.

It follows, then, that while a section of this paper should deal with the various theological lines of approach, a second section should consider the African view of man. A synthesis would seem desirable; yet a synthesis is impossible without reflecting upon the African contemporary situation from which, indeed, a synthesis is anticipated to emerge in time.

The second difficulty is with the use of the term "African". Objections have been raised from certain quarters, theological and otherwise, against the free way in which it has been used. Africa is such a large continent, composed of hundreds of peoples of several races, and it would be misleading to make general statements about "African" beliefs and practices. Those who raise the objections point, and justly do so, to the great differences that exist among Africans. To prove their point, they tend to go to extremes, shutting out the possibility that similarities, identical in many cases, do exist, and that in a real sense it is possible to talk of an "African personality", an "African way of life", and "an African approach". This, too, could be done with a bias; but fear of prejudice should not unduly bend the evidence toward the counter tendency.

The present writer does not, however, attempt to speak except of his Africa: Egypt, his homeland, the Upper Nile of the Sudan, and Kenya, where he worked and undertook the study of the African heritage. Mention will be made of particular peoples (avoiding as much as possible the term "tribe", which has acquired through misuse wrong connotations) in respect of whom particular contributions are made.

Basic Assumptions

The aim of presenting the various ways in which the subject of man was treated by theologians is *variety* rather than comprehensiveness, for it is established beyond doubt that we have, in the way of theological thinking about man, not a set, rigid doctrine, but a deposit of theological heritage open for increase and renewal. In spite of the great variety, that deposit not only represents the continuity of the theological life of the Church since her early beginnings until today, but also establishes the basic assumption that theologians did not live and think in isolation from their respective localities, age and generation. To address their contemporary situation and to make themselves understood they must have used concepts, terminology and ways of thinking accessible to them through their training and experience.

As an illustration, consider, for instance, the theology of the second century, when the young Christian community had to be on the defensive against assaults from outside and heresies from inside. One main issue was the pressing need to define the faith which led the Apostolic Fathers to treat the gospel as another law. The new converts were taught to secure the forgiveness of their sins and eternal life through meritorious works and obeying the "new law of Christ". Against the "heretics" very strong words were often used. Ignatius calls them "wild beasts, mad dogs, biting secretly". He describes sin as deadly sickness for the healing of which there is only one physician, "fleshly and spiritual, begotten and unbegotten, God in man, true life in death".[1]

Justin Martyr (second century), one of the Apologists, being

---

[1] Ignatius, *Ad Eph.* vii. 2. See Henry Bettenson, ed., *Documents of the Christian Church* (London, O.U.P., 1943), p. 42.

himself a convert from paganism to Christianity, conceives of the idea that men are by nature "children of necessity and ignorance", and that through baptism they are regenerated and become "children of freedom and knowledge". He disputes the permanent obligation of the law. Christ's unique position (Divinity) entitles Him to abrogate it. A true interpretation of the Scriptures, he said, "justifies the admission of the Gentiles into the Church without requiring them to observe the demands of the law".[2]

St. Augustine (A.D. 354–430) offers in his life a remarkable illustration of how theology is deeply influenced by the theologian's experiences. Without going into the inconsistencies of his theology, it is enough to point out that his doctrine of "irresistible grace" is the natural outcome of a life that could not avoid the claims of God. Only a man who knew the anguish of defeat in the face of his carnal lust could think of it as the root of human damnation and human loss of free will. Listen to his words of confession addressing God:[3]

I sent up these sorrowful words: How long, how long?
Tomorrow and tomorrow? Why not now?
Why not is there this hour an end of my uncleanliness?

I. ESTIMATING MAN—THEOLOGICAL LINES
OF APPROACH

Four distinct ways of approach to our subject are discernible:

a. Estimating man on the basis of the Genesis record of man's origin and sin.
b. The Christ-centred approach.
c. The social approach.
d. The evolutionary approach.

(a) *Estimating Man on the Basis of the Genesis Record of Man's Origin and Sin*[4]

Irenaeus (A.D. 120–200) maintains that man was not created in a state of perfection from the beginning, "for things which

[2] F. L. Cross, *The Early Christian Fathers* (London, Duckworth, 1960), pp. 50–52. Cp. Justin, *Dialogue with Trypho*, 109.

[3] Augustine, *Confessions*, VIII, xii, 28.

[4] For a comprehensive survey, see Sydney Cave, *The Christian Estimate of Man* (London, Duckworth, 1944).

have recently come to birth cannot be eternal; and, not being eternal they fall short of perfection for that very reason. And being newly created they are therefore childish and immature, and not yet trained for an adult way of life."

The "image of God" is explained as "incorruption"—the gift which got lost with the Fall, but restored through the Incarnation. Yet, man's fall served God's purposes to lead man into maturity.

On the nature of man, Irenaeus says, "The complete man is a mixture and a union, consisting of a soul, which takes to itself the Spirit of the Father, to which is united the flesh which was fashioned in the image of God." The soul is perceived as midway between the flesh and the spirit.[5]

Origen (c. A.D. 185–254), the Platonic theologian from the Alexandrian school, explains rationally the universality of sin in the context of the whole universe. According to him, the souls were created in the beginning and had an existence comparable to that of the angels—a state from which some have fallen and become tied to the flesh. According to the diversity of their works different states are assigned to them in this world. Some are born as human children; and some, indeed, may "reach such degradation, and forgetting their rational nature and dignity they sink down to the order of irrational beings and brutes".

The "image of God" in man is thus explained as "rational dignity", "the possibility of perfection". It is differentiated from the "likeness of God" which is reserved for the final consummation and which man must appropriate for himself by "the eagerness of his own efforts". This is possible because the Creator "granted to the intelligences the power of movement at their own free will, and that was in order that the good done in them might be their own, by being maintained by the use of their own will".[6]

From among the African writers we meet with Tertullian (A.D. 160–240?), the Stoic lawyer who found in Jesus Christ the sufficiency of knowledge. In his preoccupation with defending Christianity against Marcionism, he presented the

[5] F. L. Cross, *op. cit.*, pp. 113 ff., and Bettenson, *op. cit.*, pp. 92 ff. Cp. Irenaeus, *Adv. Haer.*, V, 16.

[6] F. L. Cross, *op. cit.*, pp. 270–280.

gospel as law. Sin is universal, he said, because man's soul is born sinful. Man has inherited Adam's body and soul, although a grain of goodness still lingers in the human soul mixed with the inherited uncleanliness. Sin committed after baptism can only be forgiven through penance and humility. Presumption is man's original sin and his most grave one.

In spite of his firm stand against the Marcionite view that creation was brought into being by the Demiurge, Tertullian could only conceive of marriage as something related to fornication, while abstinence from it is related to sanctity.[7]

St. Augustine, taken as a heretic or not, has influenced the thinking of the Church for generations. His estimate of man, while far from being consistent in all his works, makes the following points:

(1) Man's nature was created at first faultless and without any sin. All the good qualities which it still possesses in its form, life, senses, intellect, it has from the Most High God, its Creator and Maker.

(2) It was expedient that man should be at first so created as to have it in his power both to will what was right and to will what was wrong, not without reward and punishment promised.

(3) Through Adam's sin his whole posterity were corrupted in him, and were born under the penalty of death, which he had incurred. All descended from him, and from the woman who had led him into sin; being the offspring of carnal lust on which the same punishment of disobedience was visited, they were tainted with the original sin, and were by it drawn through diverse errors and sufferings into that last and endless punishment which they suffer in common with the fallen angels, their corruptors and masters, and the partakers of their doom.

(4) Children who die and to whom baptism, the bath of regeneration, was out of reach, and were thus unable to be justified, are condemned.

It is even probable that children are involved in the guilt not only of the first pair, but of their immediate parents.

(5) Man cannot restore himself to life. For when man by his free will sinned, sin being victorious over him, man's freedom of will was lost.

[7] *Tertullian: de pudicitia,* 4–5.

(6) Election rests completely with God. Part of the human race is elected and predestined for eternal life. It is only to these that God's grace is bestowed inwardly, the grace from which the beginning of faith comes.[8]

St. Thomas Aquinas (1225–1274), the Dominican theologian, successfully combined the Scriptures, Augustine, Aristotle and Neo-Platonism in one well-integrated system of thought. In many cases, he is an echo of St. Augustine, only enlarged, softened and philosophized. The following are but a few of his contributions to our subject:

There is a variety of divine resources God makes available for man, says St. Thomas. First of all, there is the grace without which man cannot inherit eternal life, nor can he in any way rise from sin. Man cannot prepare himself to receive the light of grace except by the gratuitous grace of God moving him inwardly.

In order to live righteously man needs a twofold help of God: first, a habitual gift whereby "corrupted human nature is healed". After its being healed, it is "lifted up so as to work deeds meritorious of eternal life, which *exceed the capability of nature*". Secondly, man needs the help of grace in order to be moved by God to act.

> The gift of habitual grace is not therefore given to us that we may no longer need the divine help; for every creature needs to be preserved in the good received from him. . . Man will need the divine help even in the state of glory, where grace shall be fully perfected.[9]

The differentiation between habitual grace and divine assistance is clear on the question of perseverance. St. Thomas explains perseverance in three ways: (*a*) in "standing fast lest man be moved by the assault of sadness"; (*b*) as a habit whereby man has the purpose of "persevering in good until the end". In these two, perseverance is infused together with grace, like all other virtues. (*c*) The third way is that perseverance is the "abiding in good to the end of life". In this habitual grace is not needed, only divine assistance "to guide and guard against

---

[8] Whitney J. Oates, ed., *Basic Writings of Saint Augustine*, pp. 521–579, 657–730, 790.

[9] *Summa Theologica*, Ia IIae, q. 109, art. 9 ad 1.

the attacks of the passions". Man will need to continue beseeching God for this gift, that he might be kept from evil until the *end of his life*.

Perhaps not least among the contributions of St. Thomas is his teaching that theology should take note of the circumstances of human actions. "Theologians", he says, "consider human acts under the aspect of merit and demerit, which is proper to human acts; and for this it is requisite that they should be voluntary."[10]

Martin Luther (1483–1546) sees in man's nature a resemblance to three compartments of the Tabernacle. The spirit corresponds to the "holy of holies"—"high, deep and noble, where the incomprehensible, invisible, and eternal are lodged. The dwelling place of faith and the Word of God." The soul corresponds to the "holy place" where things that could be comprehended lodge and get processed by the reason. The body is the "outer court". "Its work (with its members) is but to carry out and apply that which the soul knows and the spirit believes."

Luther's view of Adam before the Fall resembles that of St. Thomas. He explains:

> Adam was endowed . . . with a twofold life: an animal and an immortal life. The latter however was not as yet plainly revealed, but held in hope. Had he not fallen by sin therefore, he would have eaten and drunk, and worked, and generated in all innocence, sinlessness, and happiness.

Luther hesitates to give any opinion about the "image of God" after which Adam was formed. "It has been completely lost", he states, "and we can never fully attain to the knowledge of what it was." He refuses to accept that memory, mind and will compose the image of God in man. Satan has the same faculties in a much stronger form. Yet whatever it was, it was perfection and excellence, and "Adam possessed in it its moral substance".

Of original sin, he insists that it plainly appears both in "sins and in the punishment of them"; how great and terrible it, indeed, is. "Look only at lust," he contends. "Is it not most mighty, both in concupiscence and in disgust?" As a result

[10] *Ibid.*, Ia Iiae, q. 109, art. 10; q. 7, art. 2.

of the Fall, man's will and intellect became completely corrupt. The object of the gospel, hence, is seen as to restore to the origin, and indeed to a "higher image" all men, so that they may live in and with God, and be "one" with Him.

Luther believed that all men have gone out of the way, and are unrighteous, evil, sinners, and condemned. "There is nothing in man which is good." But God forgives sins merely out of His grace and for Christ's sake.[11]

John Calvin (1509–1564) is well known for reviving Augustinianism with its predestination. Calvin's theology, however, was formed under the three pressures of his personal struggle, the historic crisis of his time, and the suffering of Evangelical Christians in France. Under such circumstances, what is sought and what usually emerges is a straightforward theology with a clear-cut answer for every situation, with strong leanings towards the deterministic elements of religion, expressed in the strongest way possible. That is Calvin's theology.

Calvin sees the creation of man as the noblest and most re-markable example of God's justice, wisdom and goodness. Yet, man cannot have a clear and complete knowledge of God un-less accompanied by a corresponding knowledge of himself. The "likeness of God" extends to the whole excellence by which man's nature towers over all other kinds of living creatures. And although the primacy of the divine image was in the mind and heart, or in the soul and its powers, yet there was no part of man, in his original condition, not even the body itself, in which some sparks did not glow.

Calvin leaves no doubt that when Adam fell from that origi-nal state, by this defection, he was alienated from God. There-fore, even though we grant that God's image in man was not totally annihilated and destroyed in him, yet it was so corrupted that whatever remains is frightful deformity. Estrangement from God meant the death of man's soul. Thus, through his fall, Adam has consigned his race to ruin for he has perverted the whole order of nature in heaven and earth.

Beside general providence, God exercises especial care over each of His works, in that He so attends to the regulation of

[11] Hugh Thompson Kerr, Jr., ed., *A Compend of Luther's Theology*, Philadelphia, Westminster Press, 1943, pp. 77–89.

individual events, and they all so proceed from His set plan, that nothing takes place by chance. It is, hence, plain that the decision of God's eternal election fixes the destiny of every creature. It comes to pass by God's bidding that *salvation is freely offered to some while others are barred from access to it*. Calvin is aware of the great difficulties such an idea raises, yet his own mind is fixed on it as the revelation of God's hidden counsel. Those who cannot accept it are simply strangling themselves in darkness.[12]

(b) *The Christ-centred Approach*

Friedrich Schleiermacher (1768–1834) belongs to the group of pioneers who departed from the set pattern and who made an intellectual effort to see the human experience in its totality.[13] In this, Schleiermacher's theology is coloured by the mysticism of his Moravian background.

Schleiermacher refuses to use the Creation story as history. He declares:

> The Old Testament narrative of Creation is far from putting forward a history. Besides, history is not to be called "faith". The narrative, when it offers any help, does so in a negative way; otherwise its details raise problems because it does not tell enough, and its moral situation is not defined. . . . Thus, there is no reason why we should lay down any special doctrines concerning the first man. . . . Hence we may take it as more to our purpose not to define anything more accurately as regards the condition of the first man, but simply to elicit the ever self-identical original perfection of nature from the higher self-consciousness viewed personally. But if we are to see everything that can develop out of such original perfection all together in a single instance, it is not to be sought in Adam, in whom it must have been lost, but in Christ, in whom it has been brought again to all.[14]

It is not only his subjective universal method which is creditable, but also the unique way in which he deals with sin and grace. "Every Christian", he announces, "is conscious both of sin and grace as always combined with each other and never

---

[12] John I. McNeill, ed., *Institutions of the Christian Religion*, Edinburgh, Clark, pp. 241–264; 183–210; 920–931.

[13] Friedrich Schleiermacher, *The Christian Faith* (tr. H. L. Mackintosh and J. S. Stewart, Edinburgh, Clark, 1928) § 57.

[14] *Ibid.*, § 61.

dissociated." But for the sake of the discussion he treats them separately.

He maintains that in all of us there exists a living seed of sin ever ready to burst forth, hence there is such a thing as an abiding consciousness of sin, now preceding the sin itself as a warning presentiment, now accompanying it as an inward reproof, or following it as penitence.[15] His definition of sin is that it is an "*arrestment* of the determinative power of the spirit, due to the independence of the sensuous functions". He does not accept the traditional division between the original sin and the actual sin. If we have to use these terms, he suggests, a new relationship betwen them has to be seen.

Schleiermacher's discussion of "the corporate life" is most revealing. The appearance of Christ and His institution of the new corporate life are the completion, only now accomplished, of the creation of human nature. He explains it in this way:

> The corporate life consists solely of redeemed individuals, but it has its significance from the world only through its organization. The state of grace was called into being, along with the corporate life, or indeed before it, by the first proclamation of the Gospel.
>
> We have fellowship with God only in a living fellowship with the Redeemer, such that in it His absolutely sinless perfection and blessedness represent a free spontaneous activity, while the recipient's need of redemption represents a free assimilative receptivity.[16]

The never-ending value of the Redeemer for the community founded by Him, and the fact that redemption, the Redeemer, and the community that is redeemed can never separate in their relationship one to the other, are points of strength in Schleiermacher's theology.

Ritschl (1822–1889) followed in the footsteps of Schleiermacher in treating religious relations within the framework of the subjective life. He claims that his method is based upon "the Revelation value of Christ as the ground of knowledge for all the problems of theology". In other words, it consists in deriving everything in theology from the "pure source of revelation in the Person of the historical Christ". His main

---

[15] *Ibid.*, § 66.
[16] *Ibid.*, §§ 113–163.

thesis concerning man could be summarized in the following points:

(1) Ritschl rejects the doctrine of a government of the world by reward and punishment, because he regards it as entirely alien to the spirit of Christianity. *The error*, he maintains, must have originated from the mistaken way of *conceiving of the Divine government after the analogy of earthly states; whereas its true type is the family.*

(2) The Kingdom of God is the final end which God aims at realizing through man in the world. *Sin* can only be understood *as the opposite of this highest moral good.*

(3) Ritschl rejects the idea of an original state of innocence, and accounts for the origin of sin by the fact that man starts off a natural being, to the subject of self-seeking desires, while his will for good is a "growing quality".

(4) He rejects also the concept of "original" or "inherited" sin which, if true, he argues, would destroy responsibility, and make education impossible. Sin originates in the will, and consists only in acts of will.

(5) The world is constituted by God for His own end—the Kingdom of God, viz. that an opposed relation to this end necessarily involves man in conflict with the divine order and entails on him evils.

(6) Justification is wholly of God's free grace, the result of a "synthetic" judgement of God. This means that God does not "analytically" declare the sinner righteous by first making him so (Catholic doctrine); but by a creative act of will He gives him the relation of fellowship with Himself despite the personal sinfulness of the sinner. The justified sinner, notwithstanding the sin and guilt of his past life, or still cleaving to him, is delivered from his fears, and has trust in God awakened in him.[17]

Karl Barth's approach is Christological, yet not in the same sense as Ritschl's, for where Barth says, "the Word of God", Ritschl would say "history", consequently their roads fully part.

True to his "predominance of grace", Barth says that the only basis of man's creaturely being is the grace of God in Jesus

---

[17] James Orr, *The Ritschlian Theology and the Evangelical Faith*, London, Hodder & Stoughton, 1897, pp. 136–163.

Christ, in which is grounded all that we really know of man: who he is and what he is. As far as grace goes, we know; outside of that all that we know lies in the realm of "working hypotheses of man's self-understanding".[18] These hypotheses deal with man's biological, rational, ethical, religious, social and anthropological existence, and are all "permissible and necessary . . . but they do not solve the question of the common denominator, i.e. of man himself". Barth goes on to say:

> This question is solved, however, if we set out from the fact that man is the being to whom God is gracious in Jesus Christ. From this there result definitions which certainly do not extinguish as such or even obscure these phenomena of human existence, which do not contradict or render superfluous these working hypotheses of human self-consciousness, which give them a firm basis as hypotheses, but which, as opposed to them, refer to the realm of man, to man himself. In the fact, revealed to us in God's Word, that God is gracious to man in Jesus Christ, we do not see any of these views of man either confirmed or questioned, nor do we see any view of man, but we see man himself, what and how he really is.[19]

In this way, Barth narrows down our field of operation. We have only to see the glory of God residing in Jesus Christ, then we see man himself, "humbled, accused and judged, as a guilty and lost creature". But in the same fire of judgement, we see him "upheld, and saved . . . and exalted and glorified as the creature elected . . . for all eternity".

Barth speaks of the ontological significance of Jesus Christ, "the one man among all others". Thus, all men "are creaturely beings whom this man is like for all his likeness, and in whose sphere and fellowship and history this One man also existed in likeness with them". This relationship between the One and all the others brings with it dynamic changes, "every man in his place and time is changed, i.e. he is something other than what he would have been if this One had not been man".[20] Thus in Jesus Christ man has a human Neighbour, Companion, and Brother, without whom it is debatable that man can be man at all.

[18] Karl Barth, *Church Dogmatics*, edited by Bromiley and Torrance, Edinburgh, Clark, III, 4, p. 41.
[19] *Ibid.*, III, 4, pp. 41 f.　　　　[20] *Ibid.*, III, 2, pp. 132 f.

In the light of this relationship, the true dimensions of our sin are uncovered. "Sin itself . . . , is an ontological impossibility for man. We are actually with Jesus, i.e., with God. This means that our being does not include but excludes sin. To be in sin, in godlessness is a mode of being contrary to our humanity . . . (Man's) very being as man is endangered by every surrender to sin. And conversely, every vindication and restoration of his relation to God is a vindication and restoration of his being as man."[21]

(c) *The Social Approach*

As early as the second century, we find Clement of Alexandria (c. A.D. 150–213) developing genuine sympathies toward the so-called pagans of his time whom he tries to address, within the context of their own culture, with the Christian message.

But it was St. Thomas Aquinas who, in treating the social aspects of human life, recognized two principles as basic to it. First, the rationality of man which enables him to seek as an end the common good of all men. The second is human nature; man's essence, or man's inner dispositions, that to which he is inclined by nature. Man has an aptitude for society, a gregarious impulse that is similar to that of other social animals. Man can neither live in isolation, nor is he by himself self-sufficient in all things related to life, nor can he achieve the purpose of life except in association with others of his kind who, like himself, have a sense of good and evil. Language makes man unique, and makes it possible for him to rationally organize his life: the family, the community and the political state. The family, because of its insufficiency, leads through the community to the civil society and ultimately to the supernatural union in the body of Christ.

This organization of life in families, communities, and the state serves two immediate purposes: to satisfy the necessities of life such as existence, nourishment and education which are provided by the family. But that is not all, for the good things of life and happiness cannot be fully satisfied without the conveniences which the community and the state provide.

[21] *Ibid.*, III, 2, pp. 135 f.

The basic relationship between man and society is that of "sharing", or "exchange" and co-operation. The individual, when mature, stands responsible to society to do his part if he is to expect, and to receive, from society the benefits without which life cannot be enjoyed.

In the modern period, Reinhold Niebuhr represents the increasing attention which theology is paying to man in society. To Niebuhr we owe the reviving of the idea that man is both the child of nature and a spirit; the spiritual and the brutal together. He also pointed out the difference between man as an individual and man in the group. He explains:

> Individual men may be moral in the sense that they are able to consider interests other than their own in determining problems of conduct, and are capable, on occasion, of preferring the advantages of others to their own. . . . But all these achievements are more difficult, if not impossible, for human societies and social groups. In every human group there is less reason to guide and check impulse, less capacity for self-transcendence, less ability to comprehend the needs of others and therefore more unrestrained egoism than the individuals, who compose the group, reveal in their personal relationships.[22]

Niebuhr makes a case against the optimism of modern educators, sociologists and religious idealists by explaining that as long as there is human society there will be conflict, particularly of a political character where conscience and power meet, and where the ethical and coercive factors of life will continue to interpenetrate and work out their tentative and uneasy compromises—compromises, not the achievement of a just society, because such a hope is "impossible" and can only be approximated by those who have its vision and who do not regard it as impossible. For "the truest visions of religion are illusions, which may be partially realised by being resolutely believed. For what religion believes to be true is not wholly true but ought to be true; and may become true if its truth is not doubted."[23]

[22] Reinhold Niebuhr, *Moral Man and Immoral Society* (London, Charles Scribner's Sons, 1933), pp. xi ff.
[23] *Ibid.*, p. 81.

(d) *The Evolutionary Approach*

The Evolutionary Approach, in a real sense, is the wider approach within which the social and cultural are often formulated. Yet, because of the many intelligent thinkers who refuse to accept the theory of evolution, we shall have to treat this section separately.

Pierre Teilhard de Chardin, in his work *The Phenomenon of Man*,[24] says that evolution is a light illuminating *all* facts, and a curve that all lines must follow. Inside of the universe as one unit, man is just part of what goes on although "we are continually inclined to isolate ourselves from the things and events which surround us, as though we were looking at them from outside, from the shelter of an observatory into which they were unable to enter".

What is significant about man, inside this unity of the universe, is that in him, more than in anything else, consciousness emerges and is still emerging in fuller dimensions, for the process of evolution has not stopped. It is only in the light of this that we can understand our destiny. There is, indeed, a destiny pointing to a future. It is inconceivable to think otherwise. "Either nature is closed to our demands for futurity, in which case thought, the fruit of millions of years of effort, is stifled, still-born in a self-abortive and absurd universe. Or else *an opening exists—that of the super-soul above our souls*; but in that case, the way out, if we are to agree to embark on it, must open out freely into limitless psychic spaces in a universe to which we can unhesitatingly entrust ourselves."[25]

This is "survival" and it is collective in scope. Two questions are, in this respect, set forward for consideration:

Evolution = Rise of consciousness.
Rise of consciousness = effect of union.

"The general gathering together," explains Pierre Teilhard, "in which by correlated actions of the *without* and the *within* of the earth, the totality of thinking units and thinking forces are engaged—the aggregation in a single block of mankind where fragments weld together and interpenetrate before our eyes in spite of (indeed in proportion to) their efforts to

[24] London, Collins, 1959.　　　　[25] *Op. cit.*, pp. 231 f.

separate—all this becomes intelligible from top to bottom as soon as we perceive the natural culmination of a cosmic process or organization which has never varied since those remote ages when our planet was young. . . .

"The outcome of the world, the gates of the future, the entry into the super-human—these are not thrown open to a few of the privileged nor to one chosen people to the exclusion of all others. They will open to an advance of *all together*, in a direction in which *all together* can join and find completion in a spiritual renovation of the earth."[26]

Yet the gates of the future are perceived as having opened into the Mediterranean region, the West in particular. "It is in this ardent zone of growth and universal recasting that all that goes to make man today has been discovered, or at any rate must have been discovered. For even that which had been known elsewhere only took on its definitive human value in becoming incorporated in the system of European ideas and activities."[27]

Pierre Teilhard's vision of collective togetherness rests on his conviction of the great importance of *personality*. As man moves forward into the future, he is destined (in a sense) to cross the limits of self-consciousness to a transcended existence of integration in which he is able to meet "the other", to borrow an existential phrase. And "when we turn towards the summit, the totality and the future, we cannot help engaging in religion".

We are now passing through a period of transition in which "the present blends with the future in a world of upheaval", Pierre Teilhard points out. We are being made aware, through the pains of change, of the new forces operating in a "world come of age" (the famous words of Dietrich Bonhoeffer) in which the time of religion—the time when men could be told everything by means of words, whether theological or simply pious—is over; and so is the time of inwardness and conscience. We stand near the completion of a long development towards the autonomy of man and the world, and we are moving rapidly into a time of irreligion. Beginning as early as the secular impulses of the thirteenth century, man has more and more

[26] *Ibid.*, pp. 243 f.
[27] *Ibid.*, pp. 210 f.

been able to answer his important questions without recourse to God as a "working hypothesis".[28]

By whatever name we may call the present period—"technocratic era" according to van Leeuwen, in which "the technological revolution has reached a stage of total impasse", or "technopolis" era, in which, according to Harvey Cox, "the secular metropolis stands as both the pattern of our life together and the symbol of our view of the world"—the fact remains unchanged that all mankind, wherever they may be and at whatever stage of civilization they are, are faced as one man with one process which "nothing can either reverse or hold in check. There is no way back, but there is a way ahead," affirms van Leeuwen.

The main features of this era include among others its materialistic outlook. "Pluralism (also) is breaking out where once a closed system stood. . . . Diversity and the disintegration of tradition are paramount. . . . A type of impersonality in which functional relationships multiply . . . and a degree of tolerance and anonymity replace traditional moral sanctions and long term acquaintanceships."[29]

Nature has been disenchanted, politics desacralized, man's values deconsecrated and "shorn of any ultimate or final significance", as Cox well explains the process. But, would that mean that man is lost? Cox answers that there is no reason for alarm. In its very essence, the process is that of grace, the outcome of the biblical faith, and in which the gospel is at work as "the activity of God creating new possibilities in history."[30]

II. THE AFRICAN VIEW OF MAN

All that goes into the making of man is incorporated in the complex unity of the tribe, outside of which all others are strangers and inferiors, if not enemies. "The things of Shilluk are good, the things of the strangers are bad," runs a

[28] John D. Godsey, *The Theology of Dietrich Bonhoeffer*, London, S.C.M. Press, 1960, pp. 248–250.

[29] Harvey E. Cox, *The Secular City*, London, S.C.M. Press, 1965, p. 4. Compare with A. Th. van Leeuwen, *Christianity in World History*, London, Edinburgh House Press, 1964, ch. 8.

[30] *Ibid.*, p. 47.

common tribal saying. And when a stranger is at all taken into confidence, he is at best treated as an equal.

The origin of man exhibits, according to African traditions, one common factor: man was created by God and that he has his origin in Him. The African, like a good pragmatic, produced no theological systems to frame his beliefs. He regards God with great awe as the origin of all good and evil, and as the remote, uncomprehended Being to whom *lamo* (to conjure, pray, adore) rather than *kwaco* (to ask, beg) should be directed in worship.[31]

Even when the action of creation is seen as being delegated by God to some divinity, such as to the Ameru god of creation, *Murumbi* (the same name as that of the first Kikuyu woman), the "producing" or "bringing into existence" remains with God. This fact is expressed in the Masai language by assigning the name of God to the feminine class. God is; hence man is—that is the core of the African belief. Details might differ with the different tribes. The first man and woman might have been created under a certain sacred tree, on this or that side of a certain hill, inside a certain cave or at the foot of a certain mountain.

Man might have been inside a gourd brought out of the river by a cow. Brown or black clay, or ashes might have entered into his constitution. His early physical form may be viewed as having been different from that of his descendants. For instance, two or three generations after the creation of the first man, *Nyikang*—the most adored progenitor and divine ancestor, father, king and hero of the Shilluk people—emerges as being half man, half crocodile. His mother, *Nyakayo*, still existing somewhere about the junction of the White Nile and Sobat, appears till today from out of the water as a crocodile and chooses her own sacrifices from among the elect of people, and cattle.

This ambiguity, in a way, is to be expected as long as man belongs to the realm of the spiritual. Although he has a body, yet it is inconsequential to define with precision how it came into existence. It is a temporary residence which gets its significance from its unity with that which dwells within it. The body is the oil-container of the lamp, according to an old

---

[31] The Shilluk view expressed above represents that of many other tribes.

Egyptian saying. Once the oil is all gone, what is left is an empty shell, however precious that may be.

The Concept of Soul

What, then, is that principle, force, entity, or essence which makes of man, man? What is that "thing itself" which gets united with the body, forming with it a whole? In its state of unity with the body it is variably referred to as "heart", "head", "judgement", "mind", "reason", "soul" and "breath". When it departs it is referred to as "shadow", "ghost", "spirit", and "soul".

The Dinka language offers a good example of the present terminological difficulty. The part of man which is viewed as immortal is termed *atiap*, a word that means both ghost and shadow. It is restricted in its usage to the spirit of the dead. Yet *atiap* may be replaced by *pir* which means life, movement, or vitality, or *wei*, which means spirit, or with a slight change of accent and vowel, breath. But the centre of man's character and manners is *piou*, which means heart. This too is immortal. It is the *piou* which keeps a person alive in the memory of the community: a very important aspect of immortality as viewed by Africans.

Added to this is the fact that in Luo traditions life is emphasized as being the immortal aspect of man. Yet life is something communal. This is signified by the phrase "our life" in which the plural is commonly used to designate the life of a single individual.

From all of what we have said, it becomes evident that we are dealing with a dynamic element, not a mere entity or static being. It is something very close to being the life-essence of man which draws from the very life-essence of the universe.

In order to explain that dynamic element within the context of the total life of the African community, Father P. Tempels suggested the term "vital force" which has proved both handy and controversial. Janheinz Jahn, in particular, found in it fascinating possibilities for explaining or systematizing certain aspects of African beliefs. Granting that the process of philosophising and systematization has gone a little too far and that forcing the varying traditions into one smooth pattern could be exceedingly superficial, the idea behind the term "vital force" has helped many to grasp something of the depth and grandeur of the African viewpoint.

The main thesis of Jahn is that human individuals come into this-being as a result of cosmic "life-force" or "vital force", acting upon the biological union of "shadow" and "body" as united with the spiritual life; "for the production of a human being," he says, "is a process of body and spirit. The principle which assists in every beginning of a human creature. . . . Biological life . . . he shares with the animal, but spiritual life divides from the animal."[32]

Man in Relation

Existence-in-relation sums up the pattern of the African way of life. And this encompasses within it a great deal, practically the whole universe. The African maintains a vital relationship with nature, God, the deities, ancestors, the tribe, the clan, the extended family, and himself. Into each avenue he enters with his whole being, without essentially distinguishing the existence of any boundaries dividing one from the other. Lightning, for instance, causes the Baluhya man to gasp in awe as he watches *Were* (God) chasing *Akana* (the snake-like agent of evil) at great speed across the cloudy sky. Moreover, human ancestors and the divinities are not distinguishable.

Two basic principles seem to underlie all the complex relationships into which man enters, namely, the principle of indwelling and the principle of interaction.

· It has been noted by anthropologists that the African participates in the spirit-world. This is illustrated by the *Jok* of the Dinka people. The person on whom a certain *Jok* descends is called *wun Jok* (the owner of Jok) or *ran Jok* (the man of Jok), or still *aci Jok dom* (being possessed by Jok). His own being participates in the being of the divinity to the point at which the borderline between the supernatural and the natural diminishes.

On the other hand, a cannibal may be changed at his death into a man-eating lion. Hence a corpse is covered with an animal hide when buried. This practice may be better understood from a Bari belief that the life-essence or soul does not

[32] J. Jahn, *Muntu*, London, Faber, 1961, p. 118.

leave the body immediately after the occurrence of death. It lingers on for a while. In the case of a rain-maker, the people keep quiet until the elders have prepared a mixture of fibres from a certain sacred tree, and mud, and plastered all the openings of the corpse. In case of failure to do that, the soul might jump out and into the bush to become a leopard lying in wait to devour the village goats.

But the process of indwelling is not a one-way process. The Zande believe that each clan has its own life-carrier in the form of a small animal such as a frog or a crab. The soul or the life-essence of a dead person changes itself into the form of that particular animal, then crawls under the bed of a woman (or her daughter) of the same clan to give her a child.

Perhaps most significant in this respect is the Kikuyu practice of *guciarwo ringi*, or new birth. A person who is seriously ill plays the role of a child sitting in his mother's lap while a ceremony proceeds through which the life of a slaughtered sheep is substituted for the life-essence of the dying person.

It is also possible to discern a principle which may be stated as "the preservation of the wholeness of the universe through the interaction of its entities". Within the one communal and dynamic existence, for good or ill, man influences the individual existence of the other men, and they influence his in the same manner, through the manipulation of certain force units of the universe, such as magic. One way of accounting for this phenomenon is viewing it as the outcome of a purely subjective approach to life. In other words, man reacts emotionally, mentally and physically to what goes on around him, and hence seeks to explain what happens to him as well as to control its causes.

Sickness, for instance, is not the normal, therefore it is a threat to man's security. The possible causes are, then, to be found. Is it the wages of disobedience, disrespect, or of ignorant breaking of the tabus? Could it be a greedy ancestor or a malicious enemy that moved something from outside (such as a foreign substance or an evil spirit) to enter into the body of the sick person? The spirit-world is, indeed, operative in this situation as well as in all other situations of existence, for the spiritual is never separated from the physical. A demon-possessed body is beaten with cruelty—not to cause injury to it, but to inflict pain on the demon inside until it evacuates. Charms to cure or to render evil-proof never cease being twigs and slices of hide, but they are carriers of the spirit-principle which restores and protects.

On the one hand, what we find here is far from being a fatalistic attitude toward life. On the other hand, the African is fully conscious of the wholeness and cohesiveness of the whole creation of God, within which interaction is the only way to exist.

Father Tempels explains this phenomenon of the universal vital force. He states:

> Man is one of these resultant living forces, created, maintained and developed by the vital, creative influence of God. At his own level, man, by the divine force, is himself a living force. Man is not the first or creative cause of life, but he sustains and adds to the life of the forces which he finds below him within his ontological hierarchy. And therefore, in Bantu thought, man, although in a more circumscribed sense than God, is also a causal force of life.[33]

Gradation into Immortality

To the African, immortality is the highest good for the achievement of which his whole life is structured. He is born, brought up, trained, gradated, initiated and led into maturity so as to attain the greatest of all personal hopes.

A sample of various beliefs in immortality may be in order before we attempt a systematic classification of them.

The Chuka people refer to the dead as having "gone home". Yet the dead are expected to come back to visit their own, to bless and to punish. The community, on the other hand, keeps in touch with the ancestors through offering them sacrifices and having their names remembered by giving them to the new-born children.

The Giriama, as well as the Embu peoples, offer sacrifices on the grave so that the soul of the dead person may be able to take something along with which it may meet friends where it goes. The spirits of the dead participate in the affairs of the community, and that participation continues as long as wine and meat are offered them and their names remembered.

[33] Tempels, *op. cit.*, pp. 65 f.

According to the Akamba, the *imu* of the dead never dies. It comes back to talk to the family in dreams and to protect them from diseases and from enemies. If forgotten, the spirit of the dead becomes angry and may punish the community by destroying their crops and rendering their girls barren.

The Mbere people consider that the *ngoro* of the dead "escapes" to join the ancestors. But visiting the grave is a tabu as it annoys the spirits.

The Masai people believe that every person gives part of himself to his children. Even in his lifetime that part goes to them. The body of the dead is given over to be devoured by wild animals. If the body remains in the open for three days without its being devoured, a sacrifice may be offered with prayers so that it may be quickly finished. The spirit, though, turns into something similar to a demon. Yet, paradoxically, death is conceived of as the end of both the physical and the spiritual together.

Generally speaking, beliefs in immortality run on several levels. The pattern which seems almost always consistent is that the people who hold to the first level, mentioned below, tend to accept all the other levels with it. Where a certain level is missing in the beliefs of a people, the levels below it, not above it, are accepted. The levels run as follows:

(1) A special kind of immortality awaits people of high rank in the traditional community. They are to be close to the divinities and to accept the worship and the prayers (requests) of their subjects. The Shilluk *reth* (king) and the chiefs of several other tribes are among those who are to enjoy this type of immortality.

(2) Immortality may mean joining the ancestors and receiving, in a few cases, a new measure of life. The Anuak, for instance, say that *tier caar nyokwow* is a place where life is obtained after death. That place, however, is conceived to be around the corner, somewhere under a certain tree. This is simply extended existence in and with the community in which the person expects to continue fulfilling his role as father and guardian.

(3) A person may also extend his existence in his (in a few cases, in her) children and grandchildren in whom he is reborn.

What we have here is something more than procreation but not identical with reincarnation. The emphasis is laid on the physical, moral, and spiritual qualities of the father which reappear in the son.

(4) *Mutigairi* in Kikuyu means both "to be remembered" and "being immortal"; it is especially used of good persons. This aspect of immortality is almost common to all Africans. But the Taita people place special emphasis on the person's making a name for himself, or distinguishing himself through his works, skills, words of wisdom, and wealth. The name of such a person is often given by the Shilluk to a homestead or a village. But it is usually through stories about him or through belongings which he left behind that the person keeps alive in the memory of the community for generations.

(5) Married men alone are conceived of as immortal, for they may leave part of themselves in the younger generation. Polygamy may have been the logical application of this belief. It is possible, though, to marry a dead person *in absentia* and rear children in his name.

The Gradation Process

A new-born child is viewed by the African community both as the fulfilment and the fulfiller of the hope of immortality. Consequently he has to be brought up affectionately indeed (the Shilluk people set an example of the tender, devoted care for children), and gradated step by step into maturity. The following principles compose the framework of the process:

(1) *Life is viewed as a structure of roles and functions*

As an illustration of what is meant by this principle, consider the word "father" as used in Africa, North and South. The term applies not only to the immediate father, the procreator, but also to the paternal uncles and all the men of the clan of the father's age-group. Being a father, or an uncle, each by itself, is a distinct role, to fulfil a certain distinct function in the society, and carries with it certain obligations and rights.

The same could be said of the class of religious professionals: the medicine-man, the diviner, etc., who link up together to serve a certain function, namely watching over the physical and spiritual security and well-being of the community. Very closely linked with the function of religious professionals is that of political institutions, although both institutions are in fact religious in nature and political in exercise. The king, the chief, and the elder have the function of preserving the integrity of the community and watching over its peace and security.

Evidence is ample that when the bearers of office in the two institutions fail in their duty, the community then avenges itself ruthlessly by getting rid of the self-seeking, disloyal, greedy, or lazy organ. The king and the *kwany reth* of the Shilluk face the threat, when sick, of being strangled to death by their subjects at any moment. The witch-doctors of many a tribe meet their fatal end at the hands of their dissatisfied clients.

(2) *Grouping the community according to age defines the vertical as well as the horizontal relations within the community*

Human relationships within the traditional African society are structured and regimented. Fundamentally, there is reason to believe that the early African communities had no recognized class system. Where royalty existed, such as among the Shilluk, it was controlled by social checks and balances which restricted its power and kept the royal family renewed through systematic and continual infusion of new blood from its subjects. The Nuer and the Masai are among the many tribes who, until today, have no class system inherent in their traditions. Of the Nuer, Evans-Pritchard says that society is regimented on the basis of age-sets. "Members of the same age-set are on terms of entire equality. A man does not stand on ceremony with his age-mates, but jokes, plays, and eats with them at his ease. Age-mates associate in work, war, and in all the pursuits of leisure. They are expected to offer one another hospitality and to share their possessions. Fighting is considered an appropriate mode of behaviour between age-mates, but a man ought not to fight a man of a senior set. The comradeship between age-mates springs from a recognition of a mystical union between them, linking their fortunes, which derives from an almost physical bond, analogous to that of true kinship, for they have shed their blood together."[34]

The Kikuyu distinguish four separate stages in the process of gradation into maturity:

(a) From birth until the piercing of ears (which takes place when the child is about nine years old) the child keeps very close to his parents who train him (or her) and instruct him in community life.

(b) Once his ears are pierced the child may meet with grown-ups and sit on the council of the elders listening, but he is not allowed to participate.

(c) Circumcision takes place some time between 18 and 20 years of age. Much preparation and ceremony takes place before one age-set receives that blood symbol by which the young are initiated into the life of the adults. Boys and girls are put together for days in certain houses where they get instructed by their seniors in the matters of conduct and sex. Emphasis is laid on self-control as the most important quality in mature life.

(d) After the age of 20, that is, after circumcision, young men and young women are free to meet together in dances and in work. They are expected to choose their mates, get married and produce children fulfilling their role in community life as responsible grown-ups.

The Masai who insist on more rigorous training for their young men expect them to go, some time after circumcision, into a stage of *muranhood* or being trained as warriors in which they learn to live in camps, independently providing for themselves and practising war skills, including actual raiding and looting of cattle from other tribes.

The *murans* come out of this stage, which takes anywhere from three to ten years, with much ceremony in which hands are laid on one of their age-set, chosen through divination and the council of religious professionals with the chiefs of the tribe. That "anointed" person, from that time on, acts as the chief, adviser, counsellor, and captain of that age-set.

The removal of teeth (Baluhya practice), or marking the forehead through repeated cutting to produce bead-like figures or straight lines on it (the practice of the Shilluk, Nuer and

[34] E. E. Evans-Pritchard, *The Nuer*, Oxford, Clarendon Press, 1940, p. 257 f.

Dinka) are symbolic of the seriousness of being an adult. Pain is to be patiently endured. And for the mother who watches the operation being done on her own child this seals once for all the fact that he is the child of the tribe as well. For the members of that age-set, it is a blood-sealed covenant which is not breakable, even by death. The new adult person knows that he (or she) is now able to bear independently the responsibilities of life, being no more a child, within the context of the unity and the cohesion of the community. The most meaningful sign of that individual independence is to be able to procreate and to bear children. Pride and thrill are characteristic of the young who find in their particular sex the physical and spiritual fulfilment of both their individual and communal life.

In this connection, John Taylor shows how "step by step the child is made a member of Mankind" by gradation through rite and ceremony. In this totality marriage and sex have very distinct meaning. He explains:

> For sex is good, and the joy of it goes far beyond its physical pleasures and outshining even the shame, which may be great, of breaking the bounds. Africa has not always agreed with Europe as to what was right or wrong in this sphere, but traditionally there have always been strict controls and sanctions.[35]

(3) *The authoritarian pattern followed in the bringing-up of the young takes into full consideration the realities of human nature*

There is something in man that must be restrained and put under control: something always ready to move in the wrong direction. The Akamba say, "A good person may go astray while we look on." For this reason the parents are there to correct and straighten the young. "A home with a sharpening stone," say the Embu people, "is in a privileged position". Parents and older folk are indispensable for the moral sharpening of the young.

Yet the Africans have much sympathy with the young generation. Foolishness and ignorance are bound together, and they are expected to be in the young. The Baluhya well say,

[35] John Taylor, *The Primal Vision*, London, S.C.M. Press, 1963, p. 110.

"Had you seen your mother when she was but a girl you would have considered your father wasting his dowry on her". In other words, overlook the foolishness of the young; consider their age.

But once the young have come of age, then they are expected to heed advice. "Advise him who can be advised", says a Chuka proverb. Hence you will not need to teach a man twice that "the teeth of a dog do not lock together", or a woman that "sharing is in all things especially food".

Admittedly, the African authoritarian system produced a measure of uniformity: the individuals of whom society was made had on them an enduring stamp. But even this could be exaggerated. Individual differences were never eliminated or even discouraged. Change of the structure of society was indeed not tolerated, but individual had freedom within that structure. A woman could express her mind in the most solemn assembly of the Shilluk. She could participate in wars and lead companies of men. In dealing with disputes all parties had equal rights to speak out and no decision could be taken except when a consensus was reached. The divinities were often called upon to help find the truth before making decisions.

It was recognized, though, that the opinion of one person could be utterly wrong. In divorce cases, for instance, it was a common practice that others of the clan had as much say as the husband. He may accuse his wife of being lazy, but they may side with her against him and keep her in her home against his wishes.

(4) *Human dignity is to be preserved at all costs, for a person's dignity is part of his immortal soul or life-essence*

The African indirect approach, or the long route he takes to come to the point, has been often misunderstood, but it is the African way of keeping for the next man his dignity. You learn, through the long greetings, of his real condition. You put forward in conversation feelers to find out his reactions to the proposals you intend to introduce later on. As a host, you never ask a man whether you can do something for him. You are expected to do all you can, offering him your hospitality and warmth of reception, thus creating for him the right atmosphere to talk out his heart.

The poor of the Shilluk people are never exposed. There is no shame in poverty as long as one has done his share of the work. It is the common practice for an empty basket to be left in the centre of the village by an anonymous girl as an indication that some family is in difficulty. Spontaneously, the women of the village open their stores and put in the basket whatever they can afford to give away—sometimes from their very need. No questions are asked. The anonymous person, after a while, emerges out of the bush to lift up the full basket to her head, then she goes her way.

A neighbour, according to the Egyptian traditional custom, is more close to his neighbour than to a brother, no matter of what religion or social position the neighbour may be. He defends your uncovered back in your absence and looks after your interests when you are not aware. One major evidence of the spirit of neighbourliness is to keep for your neighbour his dignity. If he seeks to borrow from you, you give him what he needs in secret. His word is as good as a bill. In his troubles, you do not wait until he comes with them to you. In haste you make your human presence felt beside him.

The things that last

Thus, an individual is brought up and nurtured on the intricate relationships within his society, and against its background, gradated step by step into maturity. Each step brings with it more knowledge and understanding as the secrets of the universe open up gradually to his inquisitive mind. Each step brings with it, also, a greater measure of self-discipline. Only the married man, demands a Kikuyu tradition, to whom at least one child has been born, is introduced to his first drink of beer.

Advancing in years is advancing in wisdom and respectability or, in other words, getting closer to the dead. The body and soul of the elderly person grow thinner and finer to allow the life-essence to shine out and through. He may even reach a point at which an inner yearning, a small voice from beyond, takes full control of him, a compelling desire for release comes upon him. He bids his own farewell, giving them his last advice, the fruit of years of experience. Then he wraps his head with his mantle, or submits his throat to the bony hands of the old women of the village who perform the sacred duty of helping him depart. And he departs, only for a while if he departs at all, for some part of him continues to stay with his community.[36]

Death is no enemy. It is the ecstasy of fulfilment.

Yet the African views death as the disruptor of relationships. When it occurs a restoration is immediately sought. The spirit of the dead is ushered into its new state through an offered sacrifice. The ceremony includes a war cry at which the armoured men of the clan engage in imitating a battle with an imaginary foe (the custom of the Shilluk, Baluhya and others). This is done to satisfy the dead person that they are able to hold the fort and to defend the tribe against all forces of annihilation. The wife of the dead person is not allowed to give anything to, or be given anything by, anyone until a restoration of relationships is achieved through giving her in marriage to another husband.

The ethical system

The structured system of relationships is accompanied with a structured ethical system in the light of which each individual knows where he stands. Professor Idowu explains the distinctions which the Yoruba people (West Africa) make between ritual and purely ethical errors, and for which cases the offended divinities and ancestors reprimand the offender.[37]

In many cases, the offender does not stand alone in guilt. His family and, perhaps, the whole community stand with him. Mary Douglas illustrates the solidarity of the Lele of Kasai by showing that "the offence by one member affects adversely the whole village".[38] Kenneth Little, talking of the Mende of Sierra Leone, shows how, by the sin of one person, the whole family is symbolically bound up together in its guilt.[39]

What is sought is nothing less than the restoration of rela-

---

[36] The practice described is of the Shilluk kings and the males of the king's family (*Kwareth*).

[37] E. Bolaji Idowu, *op. cit.*, p. 148.

[38] Daryll Forde, ed., *African Worlds*, p. 13.

[39] *Ibid.*, p. 133.

tionships within the immediate community, for the real power of sin is in disrupting the otherwise normal flow of life and force of the universe.

Conclusions

No attempt is made at this point to put forward definite conclusions because there are none. Nor is there any attempt to reconcile or even compare the theological estimate of man, as a deposit of Christian thought, with the African traditional view, for such an attempt would be utterly superficial. The theological deposit yields clues to the trends within the Church, in many cases characterized by dialectic shifting from one pole to its opposite, as well as expressing definite trends outside of it. The African view is self-explanatory. Its integrity should be preserved by allowing it to stand on its own merits against the test of time. The theological and the African together form a small fragment of the total African situation of today in which many other views of man, typical of the pluralism of our time, simmer and beat against one another in the hope of influencing the shape of the African society of tomorrow.

There is no doubt that the pattern of life within any given society is an expression of a particular view of man held by that society. The shape of political life, for instance, rests on a particular view of man. The practices of religion are as much the outcome of its doctrine of God as of its estimate of man. There is a sense in which the doctrine of God can be viewed as an expression of a certain view of man. Evidently, wherever we may turn, the question of who man is cannot be avoided.

The African situation of today is very complex. For years past, Africa was taught to be shy and apologetic about its heritage. The coming in of Christianity and Western culture, associated with power and knowledge, pushed African beliefs into a corner where they continued to exist as of secondary or no importance but on which all nationalistic movements had to fall back for support and meaning. Beyond that stage of struggle other forces became evident on the scene: imported cultural ideas and tastes acquired by African intelligentsia; the slow, quiet influence of the school and the university, bearers of the scientific viewpoint; and the dazzling, intoxicating magnet of city life with all the emphasis it lays upon man and the machine as co-creators.

Throughout this period of Africa's history, the tendency was to supplant all that is African, leaving behind a vacuum: a dangerous emptiness. Iconoclastic fever swept over the continent and did tend to damage the good and bad together. The Church was the first iconoclast, the school followed, and the city picked upon what escaped smashing by the preceding two. No wonder, then, if the traditional African identified the Church with the God of the foreigner, the school with social disruption, and the city with the run-away harlot. And here we are: plurality and nothingness at one and the same time.

The African finds himself lost in the pluralism of today. He is often worried when people seem to be unable to agree because of so many different and conflicting ideas thrown on the platform. The same uncomfortable situation exists with the Church, now his Church—a situation of division which he often explains either on conscience or, more often, as mere accident. He is lost also in the impersonality of today's relationships from which he takes refuge in tribalism, an institution of a mixed blessing: on the one hand it softens any severe measures that could have been taken against political opponents, and on the other it is possible to exploit it in self-seeking interest.

The situation of the common African has not been helped by the prevailing paradox characteristic of modern life. The African entered into this age in leaps. The whole landscape was brought to his attention almost all at once. After the first shocks he was anticipating order and reason. Instead, he found an age of fast travel, but with tightened borders; an age of ecumenicity but with tightened nationalism; an age of collectivism, but with increased individual isolation; an age of rising standards of living, but with a tendency to slide into slums; and an age of plenty, but with nation-wide starvation. The African questions the logic of the whole thing.

Has the African something to say about it all? What is happening seems to affirm some of his traditional views. He has always believed that the margin between man and the brute, on one side, and man and the divine on the other, is very thin indeed. You may expect the worst of man, yet you may expect also great things, for his potential for good is unlimited. Human ideals may be illusions and dreams. But the African knows of dreams that made a great difference to him. Let man continue to dream. He may in the end realize them.

The material seems today to be the god of this age. Yet the African knows from long experience that the material holds no real, lasting satisfactions. It is only through its uniting with the ethical and spiritual, when it is subjected to the common good, that it takes on taste and meaning. Man himself is worth something, and his dignity should never be sacrificed to the material.

Power is conceived by the African as something pertaining to the divine. Hence it cannot be placed into unexercised hands. But the hands are rarely exercised nowadays. Scheduled education has replaced experience and has toppled the accepted standards. Seniority of age does not mean much any more, and a father may now be instructed by the child of his bowels. Nevertheless, power is dangerous and it kills. Like a live coal from upon the very altar of God, it can only be cared for by those who have been gradated into maturity.

6

THE THEOLOGICAL BASIS OF ETHICS

A study of the ethics of dynamism

DR. PARRINDER has observed that "the morality of the peoples of West Africa is largely indicated by the taboos, with which their lives are surrounded".[1] He is more cautious than other foreign observers of the African scene who have roundly declared that the African has no sense of sin. Even a wholly sympathetic and well-informed scholar as Dr. Edwin Smith was only able to say: "It would seem that in general Africans are not conscious of any direct relation between their theism and the ethic of dynamism—all that we mean by tabu."[2] Dr. Parrinder is in no such doubt on the issue: "The morality of West Africa is entwined with religion, for the people undoubtedly have a sense of 'sin'."[3]

Everywhere in Africa, morality is hinged on many sanctions. But the most fundamental sanction is the fact that God's all-seeing eyes scan the total areas of human behaviour and per-sonal relationships. God is spoken of as having eyes all over "like a sieve" (*Al'oju-k'ara bi-ajere*). Those who do evil in the dark are constantly warned to remember that God's gaze can pierce through the darkness of human action and motive. An *Ifa*[4] myth finishes on the note, "You who dive down as if under water to steal, though no earthly king may have seen you, the king of heaven sees". The same idea is expressed in the Yoruba poem quoted by Paul Radin in his *Primitive Religion:*

[1] E. G. Parrinder, *West African Religion*, London, Epworth Press, 1949, p. 199; 1950, p. 22.
[2] Edwin Smith (ed.), *African Ideas of God*, London, Edinburgh House Press, 1950, p. 22.
[3] E. G. Parrinder, *op. cit.*, p. 199.
[4] *Ifa* is the Yoruba oracle deity.

Its Nature and Origin:

The sun shines and sends its burning rays down upon us,
The moon rises in its glory.
Rain will come and again the sun will shine.
And over it all passes the eye of God.
Nothing is hidden from Him.
Whether you be in your home, whether you be on the
  water,
Whether you rest in the shade of a tree in the open,
Here is your master.

Did you think because you were more powerful than some
  poor orphan,
You could covet his wealth and deceive him,
Saying to yourself "I cannot be seen"?
So then remember that you are always in the presence of
  God.
Not today, not today, not today!
But some day he will give you your just reward
For thinking in your heart
That you have but cheated a slave, an orphan.[5]

For our present purpose, however, what is important is to examine the ethic of dynamism to which Dr. Edwin Smith refers
in the statement quoted earlier above.

First of all, why describe African ethic as the ethic of dynamism? We owe the description of the basic idea behind the
phrase to Fr. Placide Tempels who, in his treatise *Bantu
Philosophy*, has identified the supreme value in African thought
and pursuit as life-force, or vital force. He avers that the purpose and end of the wide range of human activities is "to
acquire life, strength or vital force, to live strongly, that they
are to make life stronger, or to assure that force shall remain
perpetually in one's posterity".[6] Illustrations have been
adduced to show that this vital force is the object of prayer
to God and of communion with ancestors. The *summum bonum*
of life, the only kind of blessings which God bestows, is possession of the greatest amount of vital force; similarly the greatest

---

[5] Paul Radin, *op. cit.*, pp. 18–19.
[6] *Op. cit.*, p. 30.

good that one can do to another is to make it possible for him to possess in an increasing magnitude the vital force.

One respect in which Christian thought under the influence of Greek philosophy differs from African thought is with regard to this conception of what being is. Western thought holds a static, while Africa holds a dynamic, conception of being. Western thought revels in abstract ideas: the African, on the other hand, prefers to grapple with reality through word-pictures, verbal imageries and concrete ideas. The suggestion has been made that it is fundamentally this which inhibits a number of pagans from allowing themselves to be converted to Christianity, the fear that they will have to give up ritual practices and habits of life which are intended to make it possible for the individual, and indeed for society at large, to acquire vital force. What has been said of conversion can be equally said of the ethical sense, ethical judgement and moral pursuit: they are all related to the people's idea of what being is. Not until one has understood that for the African "the ontologically good is the ethically good" can one appreciate and understand the moral sense of the African and the direction of ethical pursuit. Failure to perceive this may have contributed to the general denial to the African of a sense of morality. It may also have been responsible for the fact that the study of the ethics of African peoples has been considered by many a scholar to be not worth the trouble because, as they assume, the material is non-existent. In fact, of all the aspects of the relationship between Christianity and African traditional religion, the moral issue is the one on which the least amount of work has hitherto been done. Ethics is a discipline by itself, but there are not many scholars who have given attention to the ethics of African peoples.

There are two issues involved here, and they are better kept separate and distinct. The first is that far too many scholars have too quickly made up their mind that the African has no sense of sin. The second is the assumption that African religion has no ethical content. These two issues must be examined in any consideration of the theological basis for ethics, though the latter is more easily treated than the former, the general line of treatment being an examination of the ethical content of the God-idea, a survey of religious and cultic sanctions, and an

analysis of particular virtues and vices. Yet, in the final analysis, the determinative question is whether the people have an
inherent sense of morality or not, and if they have, of what
nature that sense is; whether they have a sense of sin or not,
and of what nature and significance they consider sin to be.
If the contention of Fr. Tempels has any validity at all, it
makes it essential that we should look in another direction of
ethical enquiry and see if in truth there is anything to be said
for an ontological morality among our people.

Furthermore, an attempt at a systematic outline of the theological context and basis of personal and social morality within
African traditional religion does raise the question of the permanent validity of such a basis. Contemporary society has witnessed a continuing disintegration of the structure of the old
society and a weakening of the religious beliefs and practices
cherished in the old communities. While we continue to trace
out how particular moral sanctions spring out of the cult of
particular gods and ancestors, the cults themselves disintegrate
with the disastrous effects which many observers have noted
on individual and public morality. It should be evident from
this that there is a limited value in asserting here the unity of
society and religion, and the dependence of morality on the old
religious beliefs.

It becomes important then to get our methodology right. It
would appear some cautious scholars have started to realize this.
For example, the passages quoted above from Dr. Parrinder's
work come from the first edition of his *West African Religion*
published in 1949. The second edition published in 1961 carefully omitted those passages, and, indeed, no longer contains
any attempt to make an evaluation of the morality and ethical
awareness of the people. Our study will therefore depart from
the traditional pattern of analysing the theological basis of
ethics and consider whether we cannot discover a way of treating the ethics of African peoples as "ontological, immanent
and intrinsic morality". We have chosen the Yoruba people of
Western Nigeria for a case-study with the hope that a similar
analysis can be made in other ethnic situations, and that perhaps further evidence will be forthcoming from such situations
to strengthen our conclusions.

In Yoruba religious thought, the term *Iwa* stands for both

being and morality. This *Iwa* is a permanent preoccupation in the total religious system. The whole of religion is completely involved in the realization of *Iwa*. It has become a version of *dunamis* as a predominant religious quest behind every rite, sacrifice, and prayer. In family ancestor-cult, the worshipper dips his hand in water, then touches the ground thrice saying,

Ilẹ mo pe ọ o, (thrice)	O earth, I invoke thee,
Ẹjọ kọ o,	Not to lay a charge against thee,
Iwa ni mo ntọrọ.	*Iwa* is my quest.

Having said that, he proceeds to express his wishes and petitions. In many *Ifa* oracles, we meet the same combination of a quest and a promise. For example, *Eleremoju*, the mother of *Agbọn-ni-regun* (a praise-name of *Ifa*) was given an oracle and asked to make some sacrifice to the end that her *Iwa* may be propitious (*Iwa re a su're*). *Ogundameji*, one of the oracles, speaks of *Ogun* being sent to the earth to fashion or lay the path for *Iwa*:

Agoro ọwọ ko ṣe f'apo kọ
L'o da fun Ọlọfin nigbati Ọlọfin Ajalọrun
Nran Ogun ọmọ rẹ wa sinu aiye lati wala ọna Iwa.

The elbow is not curved enough to hang a bag on
Being the oracle for Olọfin when he, Ọlọfin Ajalọrun
Was to send Ogun his son into the earth to lay the path for *Iwa*.

Another Oracle in the same group predicted to *Ogun* that the whole world would be running after him beseeching him to re-form their *Iwa*. The calabash in which the *Ifa* guardian spirit is kept is also called either *Igba Odu* or *Igba Iwa*, that is, the calabash for *Iwa*. The earliest beginning of time is also spoken of in terms of *Iwa*; e.g. *Ni ipilẹṣẹ Iwa ni Ile-Ifẹ nigbati Oduduwa da aiye*; i.e. At the outset of *Iwa* in *Ile-Ifẹ* when *Oduduwa* created the earth (or *N'igba iwa ṣẹ*, i.e. when *Iwa* originated).

Since *Iwa* is so fundamental in Yoruba thought that the beginning of time is associated with it, the present aspiration and activities in life bound up with it, and the hope of the future involved in the acquisition or the achievement of it, it becomes then very important to investigate what this *Iwa* is. But since *Iwa* as morality is related to *Iwa* as being, the former becomes an outgrowth of physico-psychical ideas. It is therefore necessary to examine in what ways ethical and psychical ideas are attributed to and derived from the body or parts of the body. We begin with the head.

There is a story told as to how the head was created. It is described literally as the story of the moulder of the head. The fact that there is no mythical story told about the creation of any other part of the body in particular apart from the head is in itself significant. It is due to the important role it plays as a theme in shamanist theology. This role is so important that the head is very frequently taken to stand for the person or personality. The story of the creation of the head can then be taken as an alternative narrative of the creation of man. Because of this importance of the head representing the person, a cult of the head has developed, known as *Iponri* or *Oluṣepin*. The latter name suggests the determiner of a man's circumstances or fortunes in life. Sacrifices may be offered to the head. This is to be distinguished from the "washing of the head" (*wiwẹ ori*) in which the head is merely an object which at present may be evil or impure and which can be rendered ceremonially clean and pure by washing it; the place of this washing in moral reform will be referred to later. In the cult of the head, however, the head is treated as personalized and therefore fit to be propitiated, cajoled or soothed. The similarity of this to the cult of Luck or Fate as understood and practised by ancient Greeks is without doubt,[7] except that the importance attached to it among the Yoruba extends beyond predestination to being and morality.

At the birth of a child, the character of the head is "sought", "heard", and known on the third, seventh, or eighth day, as the case may be. The ceremony is conducted by an *Ifa* priest or the diviner of the family deity, or failing either of the two the head of the family consults the ancestors by the simple process of casting lots with kola-nuts. When this ceremony of "hearing" the head has been properly conducted, the process reveals a number of tabus which the owner of the head consulted must observe and keep. Before the child grows up, the parents are expected to keep the tabus for the child. These

[7] Meyer Fortes, *Oedipus and Job in West African Religion*, Cambridge U.P., 1959, pp. 13 f.

may, in some cases, include the usual food tabus or some kind of vocational guidance. But the more important tabus of the head are moral in character. It appears the diviner frequently uses his common sense, and knowledge of the ancestry of the child, with particular reference to the moral weaknesses of those ancestors. Some practical wisdom is displayed here. A simple moral code of behaviour is drawn up for the individual concerned and then imposed on him on the authority of his head, nature or ground of being. There are those who have been told that their heads do not approve of anger, theft, pride, jealousy, rivalry, or even polygamy. Those who keep them have been known to protest, "My head does not permit fighting".

The head is also the avenger spirit, "catching" those who have wronged the owner of the head. It brings about their downfall; it pushes them to do evil or leads them to their death. One of the names compounded from the head is *Oriyomi*, "the head has delivered me"—it may be from danger, or from the machinations of the evil *orisa*.[8] Should *Esu*[9] or an offended ancestor be bent on doing injury to the person, the head may interpose to deliver the person. Also, when a person has done wrong, his head may deliver him from punishment. In this way, the head has been personalized and made active for the owner's good. Inasmuch as a person who is fit to bear the name *Oriyomi* is distinguished by acts of bravery and courage, it may be suggested that here the head becomes a personalization of one's natural tendency. The head thus becomes the spring of action. In the words of Dr. Parrinder, "The head is the seat of decision, will, pride. An active man has an ardent head, a tenacious man is hard-headed."[10]

If a person's head is spoken of as "hard", one meaning of this is that the head-spirit is so powerful as to be impregnable against the assaults of the enemy. It is also possible to strengthen one's head-personality and so render it unassailable by the use of devices and rites known as *madarikan*. Literally, it suggests that when the evil force goes about cutting off other people's

[8] God or divinity, as distinguished from the Supreme Being.

[9] A divinity usually regarded as mischievous, but sometimes invoked for favours.

[10] E. G. Parrinder, *West African Psychology*, London, Lutterworth Press, 1951, p. 23.

heads, *madarikan* prevents it from coming to one's turn. The head fights for the owner while the evil force is still at a distance, and either vanquishes it altogether or diverts it to some other target. But warnings are always issued to all users of *madarikan* that the power of the *madarikan* may become so "heady" as to become blind and indiscriminate, and consequently ward off good fortune, success, and goodness. One reason frequently suggested for this is that the owner of the head, trusting in the power of the *madarikan* to ward off evil, becomes so sure of himself and so forgetful of the rights of others as to neglect the moral demands made by society.

The verb *ro ori*, meaning "to consider the head", has an ethical connotation which is generally appealed to when a person has got to the stage just described. *Ro ori* is to think or reason about one's life. To think of the head is to take one's life into consideration in action and in human relationships. The man whose behaviour is unseemly, or who disobeys orders, refuses to go by the guidance of those who are older than himself, steals or tells lies, does not consider his head. The man who shuns evil ways and does that which is right has considered his head, he has thought over the several good things which he has chosen prenatally. As he may very well express it, he acts in this way "because of what I have to do on earth". On first hearing, this sounds like prudential ethics. But in fact it works out as morality based on the ground of one's being. It is a perfectionist command that says, "Do such things as will lead to the fullest development of your personality". This may be made clearer from an examination of the dialectic involved in the following statements:

Ohun gbogbo lọwọ ori	All depends on the head
Ori ni gbogbo nkan	All depends on the head
Ẹda ni gbogbo nkan	All depends on one's creation
Ayanmọ ni gbogbo nkan	All depends on predestination
Iran ni gbogbo nkan	All depends on heredity
Iwa ni gbogbo nkan	All depends on character

Here the head is interpreted in terms of mode of creation, natural tendencies, lot or predestination, the hereditary factor in ancestor-cult and social environmental forces influencing the behaviour and chances of the individual. And, in the final analysis, it is asserted that a man's circumstances in life depend on his character. The head has been treated not only in terms of such forces over which man has no control, but also, and finally, in terms of the will and personal character of the individual. Character, then, is understood as obedience to the gods, readiness to perform the appropriate rites at the right moments, a humble participation in primordial reality through the re-enacted myths. The shaman gives to these more than what we would call mere religious or superstitious rites. They have religio-ethical qualities. They are signs of obedience, humility and faith. It is an assertion that in spite of prenatal destiny, heredity, natural tendencies and the like, the man who does the will of the gods will be victorious over the elemental forces of the universe.

Sometimes, a second head is spoken of as residing inside the external head, and therefore invisible. *Ori inu* or the internal head is generally identified with character. A person may stand the chance of success or good fortune, which would be the mark of his external head, but if his character is bad, that is if he is unsociable, irascible, proud, disrespectful, ruthless, greedy of gain, then it is said that his internal head corrupts his external head; that is, his character ruins his chances of good fortune.

The internal head and the external are sometimes spoken of in collocation with each other, though the external head is not always so specifically referred to. In such cases, character is substituted for the internal head and contrasted with the external head. Thus: *Ori dara, iwa l'o ku*, meaning "As for the head, it is good, what remains is character". Head here means the external head and character is the internal head. This saying refers to one whose external circumstances are propitious, of whom it might even be said that he has a good luck, i.e. a good physical head; but his internal head, i.e. his character, is not good. A cultic rite may be prescribed for the person to "reform his head", that is his internal head, his character. This rite almost invariably includes the use of some herbs called *ewe alaşiwalu* which is the esoteric name for various kinds of leaves believed to have the power "to bind his existence together" or "to integrate character".

It is interesting to note that there is a good use made of suggestibility and religious moralization in this effort to reform the head and thereby integrate character. The *ewe alaṣiwalu* is put into fresh water drawn from the river very early in the morning, and rubbed together in the water; the *Ifa* powder on which has been inscribed the *Odu* (oracle) that refers to a good head may be blown on the water, and the owner of the head is made to wash his shaven head with the liquid, beating the head and confessing his past faults in the process, making prayerful resolutions of the way of behaviour he hopes to adopt subsequently. Then the priest winds up the ceremony by exhorting him further towards the observance of particular moral tabus in the name of the gods.

Now we proceed to examine the place of the stomach in this physico-ethical system. The stomach (i.e. the internal organs as a whole) is given such psychical attributes as emotion, intelligence, wisdom and morality; hence the verb *ro'nu*, which literally means to stir the belly or the inside. This verb has emotional association in the idea of being sorrowful or merely being depressed and moody. The same word may mean to think, consider, give thought to, or ponder over.

A person whose behaviour is unseemly and indecorous is described as *alaironu*, one who has no stirring of the stomach. For lack of this "stirring", he becomes ill-adjusted to society and life in general, his character becomes unacceptable in social life, and it may be necessary for him to perform special cultic rites or get initiated into a religious system to stir his stomach. This is one of the reasons why one goes into the *Ifa* cult. An oracle which speaks of such an initiation to the *Ifa* cult makes this clear:

> *Ainọgbọn ninu,*
> *Ail'ero n'ikun,*
> *Aini'wa rere,*
> *Ni mu 'ni wọ 'gbo-'du lẹmẹta;*
> *A ti tẹ ọ tan,*
> *K'o lọ tun 'ra rẹ tẹ.*

> For lack of wisdom inside,
> For lack of a stirring of the stomach,
> For lack of good character,
> A man goes into the *Odu*-grove thrice over

for initiation.
You have been initiated,
Now initiate yourself.

Those are the closing words in a ceremony of initiation into a cult. The initiate has to justify his initiation by good behaviour; otherwise he would have to undergo the ceremony again later on.

At this juncture, reference might be made to the idea of an agent of thought and wisdom regarded as residing in the stomach. This is called *Iye inu*, the aliveness of the stomach. When a person has temporarily lost consciousness, he regains it through the stirring of his *Iye*, the spirit of intelligence which resides within him (*Iye rẹ sọ*). When a melancholic wakes up to the need for action rather than brooding over his ills, his *Iye* has stirred. When a learner does not recollect easily, he may take an *Isọye*, a medical preparation to stir his *Iye*. To doubt is to have a double *Iye*, and this may also express itself in anxiety and lack of faith. Thus, *Iye* has a wide signification covering consciousness, thought, memory, wisdom and emotional attitudes.

Of most importance, however, is its moral use. It is usually said in reference to a disrespectful, socially maladjusted child: *Ẹni t'o bi 'mọ ti ko bi iye, ọmọlangi l'o bi*, meaning, "A person gives birth to a child having no *iye*, it is not a child; it is a mere doll". This is a play on the double meaning of *Iye* as consciousness and as ethical awareness. One who lacks this moral awareness is like a doll which has no life. One is not a person without moral consciousness, which makes one a new being, raises one to a new level of existence. To plead with a person "to reserve consciousness in the inside" (*f'iye de'nu*) is to implore him to know what he is doing, to be aware of the moral implications of his behaviour, to exercise moral judgement.

All these ideas stem from the simple verb *ro'nu*, to stir the stomach. *Ro'nu* may also carry the idea of conversion. The longer form of the verb makes this clearer. *Ronupiwada* is to give a moral consideration to one's life and change one's character. It is assumed here that to have an understanding of what one ought to do after due thought can in itself enable one to change one's character.

One who has a bad inside (*inu buruku*) is one prone to violent anger, not ready to forgive, or heed expostulation to that effect. It is said that such a one will suffer misery; hence, *inu buruku, ogun oṣi*, "A bad inside is the magical formula for getting misery".

An *oṣonu*, one who has a stubborn inside, is ill-natured, surly or peevish. He is an irascible, implacable person, liable to violent storms of anger. He is one who has a dark (black) inside where all kinds of evils lurk. On the other hand, to have a good inside is to be merciful and kind, taking the initiative to do good and to help the needy, to be considerate, feeling sympathy with the other man, able to suffer with or for him. To have a clean inside is to bear no grudge, no malice, no ill-feeling.

The belly or stomach or inside is therefore regarded as the seat of moral faculties: from there all moral impulses proceed. The most distinctive feature of the stomach, the seat of morality, seems to be its hiddenness, its being inside the body. So, reference to the moral inside speaks of the hidden depths of human nature. Morality is regarded as that which cannot be plumbed, but which alone can spring out in its own way to reveal itself either in pleasing characteristics which delight others or in bad-tempered reactions which offend others and lead oneself to social misery.

As regards the heart (*ọkan*), the word, to begin with, is used primarily for emotional states of consciousness. To have one's heart gone bad (*ọkan rẹ bajẹ*) is to be sorrowful, for example at the arrival of some bad news or at being confronted with public discovery of one's errors and offences. In this case the one who, having done wrong, shows sorrow, and whose heart is therefore said to have gone bad, implies by look and expression that he regrets having done wrong. It is genuine sorrow for one's errors that is meant here, not regret for having been found out.

To have a heart (*ni ọkan*) idiomatically means to be capable of suppressing or hiding one's sorrow. This is understood as a kind of emotional courage distinguishable from the courage that does not fear physical danger. The latter is expressed by reference to the chest (*aiya*—the verse in Proverbs 28.1, "The wicked flee when no one pursues, but the righteous are bold as a lion" is rendered: "but the righteous have a chest like that of the lion"). When one has been startled, one restores oneself by saying, "Come back, my chest, you'll have a cowrie for an offering". But when the heart shakes or trembles (*ọkan mimi*), that is when one is afraid, it is not the fear of approaching danger, it is the fear of being let down by another. When a person suspects a friend of disloyalty, "his heart trembles" (*ọkan rẹ mi*) that the friend might not keep the promise on which depends happiness or well-being. The emotion of the heart, then, as distinct from that of the chest, has a moral quality in interpersonal relationships.

Conscience is denoted as "the witness of the heart" (*ẹri-ọkan*). The man who tells a lie is reminded that his heart is witnessing against him. A prick of the conscience is spoken of as a prick of the heart. In the casting of lots, ordeal ceremonies or oath-taking, no one dares to take the diviner's potion whose heart does not assure him that he is in the right; he must be one who can stand face to face with his heart (*ẹniti ọkan rẹ da l'oju*).

Other moral references to the heart which may be quoted in brief are the following: a black heart stands for wickedness, a white heart for peacefulness, a clean heart is of one who owes no grudges, a hard heart is self-willed, a soft heart is amenable to reproof and correction, a high heart is ambitious, a light heart carries no burden of animosity. Intellectual, volitional, purposive and affectional significations of the heart also abound, but they are not of as much importance as the ethical allusions.

The complete body is used in a comparatively few moral instances. To be gentle and meek is to put one's body on the ground (*farabalẹ*), presumably from the idea of resting lying down. *Iwarapapa*, which means to agitate the body violently, is used of gluttonous eagerness. *Ilara*, the splitting of the body, refers to jealousy and envy. Jealousy is the opposite of receiving another with open arms; extreme splitting of the body drives one into extreme wickedness like becoming a witch (*Ilara alaju ni mu wọn gb'ajẹ*). *Ija ilara*, meaning a misunderstanding arising out of envy, is said to last long.

A number of these ethico-psychical attributes to parts of the body have a universal reference, but in the case of the Yoruba here investigated, the close connection with origins in mythical situations is clear from our earlier study of the head. Stories abound pointing out how parts of the body acquired moral connotations in primordial situations, e.g. how a misunderstanding arising from the envy which was originally "the splitting of the body" of some deities could not be resolved for a very long time, or how a heavy heart *in illo tempore* became light only when it shed its burden of animosity. In all these instances, morality is bound up with being: a man's mode of existence is bound up with his character; only a narrow line divides the two. The benediction pronounced by the Ancestor-Masquerade at the close of every New Year celebration imperceptibly passes from wishes for continued existence to wishes for moral well-being:

> *Odọdun l' ẹwa wa: O ma wa (Aṣẹ).*
> *Ẹsẹ-ntẹlẹ rẹ ko ni bi araiye ninu,*
> *Iwa rẹ ko ni bajẹ loju Olọdumare.*
> *Ṣebi iwa l'ẹwa ọmọ enia;*
> *O ni tẹ l'oju ọmọde,*
> *O ni bajẹ lọwọ agbalagba,*
> *Iwa rẹ yio toro bi omi af'orọ-pọn (Amin).*

> Beans be annually: you will be (Amen).
> Your footsteps will not make witches angry,
> Your being will not decay before the Supreme Being.
> Character is beauty for man.
> You will not be brought to ridicule before children,
> You will not degenerate before adults,
> Your character will be still and clean like water
>   drawn from the river in the morning (Amen).

The participant in the New Year dramatized festival goes forth into the future with the phrase *Iwa l'ẹwa* ringing perpetually in his ears. *Iwa l'ẹwa* is capable of primary, intermediate and secondary meanings, each of which is brought out at different times and with different stories by the shaman. Firstly, a fundamental and primary sense: "Being (*iwa* or *wiwa*) is beauty." Secondly, an ethical theory that "Character (*iwa*) is beauty". But midway between these two senses there arises a third meaning deriving from the double interpretation of which both *iwa* and *ẹwa* are each capable. *Iwa,* as already observed, is either being or character, while *ẹwa* is either being or beauty.

Iwa l'ęwa is therefore capable of the meaning "Being is character", or conversely "Character is being". Arranged in a syllogistic form:

> Being is beauty
> Character is being (existence), therefore
> Character is beauty.

Thus, in Yoruba thought, reality is fundamentally considered as right or wrong. The moral sense has sought to find a basis for morality in a metaphysical rationalism, the mythical explanation of which is now almost completely lost. Reality is chiefly considered from a moral point of view. Good and bad are predicates of existence. A moral evaluation of reality is the fundamental outlook. It is part of the total spiritual or animistic temper which is the ontological outlook of the people. Being is spiritual. Morality is the essence of spirituality. The fundamental nature of existence is moral. Moral law is the fundamental law of reality. Being in itself is moral. In so far as it is regarded as beauty, being is beauty; to be is to be beautiful, and to be beautiful is to be. To be not beautiful is to cease from being, and beauty is interpreted in moral terms.

With the single word *iwa*, the Yoruba sum up ideas of being and of morality. On the one hand, *iwa* speaks of existence, availability, and reality; on the other hand, it speaks of character, conduct, habit, and morality. The one suggests metaphysical, the other ethical, ideas; the one deals with ontological and psychological states, the other with moral values; the one denotes the idea of individual and corporate being, the other of both private and social morality. On the one hand, it speaks of an individual as existent, on the other hand, it examines the action of the individual both generically as character and specifically as conduct.

The concept of *iwa* passes judgement on both character and conduct with reference to their rightness or wrongness. And to the Yoruba this is exactly the same as passing judgement on being as tending towards good or evil ends.

The Yoruba word which has been used in the Bible to translate the word 'sin' is *ęsę*. Literally, it means "that which happens", and it carries a meaning which is different from that of sin as disobedience towards God. It describes not the nature of the act, but the quality of its sequel. It recognizes sin as an evil, upsetting the equilibrium of society or of personal relationships. The effects of sin also extend into the cosmic realm. Because of sin, something happens here, and also there: cosmic order can be disturbed by that which happens here. This definition of sin from the point of view of its consequences must have belonged to the stage when man just wondered about the badness of sin without being able to account for it. This is not surprising in view of the fact that we are dealing with an animistic situation which not only personalizes inanimate objects, but also assumes the presence of unseen spiritual powers working for man's ill. That attitude of mind is preserved in some non-moral, non-religious turns of phrase: *Awo fọ lọwọ mi*, "the plate breaks in my hand" for "I have broken a plate"; "the key loses itself" (*kọkọrọ sọnu*) for "I have lost the key". Sin was probably originally spoken of in such terms.

To sin (*gba ẹṣẹ*) is to appropriate the evil way of an evil power, it is to identify oneself with sinfulness. The parallel phrase *da ẹṣẹ* seems to be a higher concept. It means "to create sin". Thus man is ultimately made personally responsible for bringing about sin. He is himself the author, the inventor, the creator of sin.

It is noteworthy that in the context of sin as that for which the individual is personally responsible, the word *ẹṣẹ* has become more prevalent than such expressive terms as *aito* (that which is not fair, not straightforward), *aiye* (that which is not fitting), and *aṣiṣe* (a mistake). *Aṣiṣe* does not even carry as much ethical judgement as *aito* and *aiye* which are frequently linked together. None of the three, however, is as prevalent for expressing moral judgement as *ẹṣẹ*. When, say, a child is cruel to an animal pet, the mother may be heard to day, *Ẹṣẹ l'o ngba yẹn o*, that is, "You are identifying yourself with evil". There is a lot of gossiping and back-biting in every village, particularly among women. When a woman back-bites or speaks maliciously about another woman, anyone who believes the absent woman to be innocent of the evil spoken against her can say, *Ẹṣẹ l'o ngba yẹn o; ko si nihin, ẹlẹda rẹ wa nihin*: "You are identifying yourself with evil; that woman is not here, but her creator (her head or guardian spirit) is here." *Ẹṣẹ* has become, no doubt, the unrivalled and classic Yoruba word for that which is morally wrong.

That which must not be done is called *ewo*. Altogether, it carries today the negative idea of a "thou shalt not". It bears relationship to that which is customarily not done; no one does it. This is the idea of a tabu; indeed, tabu appears to be the original idea, especially as the word has the same root and tonal quality as *ọwọ* (that which is treated with respect and care). We have quoted above Dr. Parrinder's judgement that the tabus largely indicate what morality is in West Africa. What he did not call attention to is the fact that the tabu (*ewo*) prohibits indiscriminately, both morally and a-morally. The Yoruba doctine of morality or sin, then, does not lie exclusively in the tabu notion; Dr. Parrinder's own treatment of the matter under the headings of Personal Taboos, Taboo Words, and Royal Taboos justifies this conclusion,[11] though he did not draw it. What is important to note is that the Yoruba tabu idea has an underlying agreement with the idea of sin as that which causes evil to happen. For example, when a child inquires from his mother why he should not do a particular act, the only explanation given by the mother is *ẹwo ni*; that is enough to stop the child. This not because *ewo* carries the idea of prohibition, but because it says the act is capable of producing evil.

Nwọn ni 'Ewo ni, a ki jẹ igun'; Iwọ ni baba tirẹ jẹ ẹ ri.
Baba rẹ na nkọ bayi? O ti ku.
Iwọ mọ bọya igun ti baba rẹ jẹ l'o pa a?
'Tis said "Tabu, we don't eat the vulture". You reply your father ate it before.
And where is your father? He is dead.
Do you know whether your father died for eating a vulture?

The myth behind it is closely parallel to the story of Adam and Eve in the Garden of Eden. But it is not the disobedience that is emphasized so much as the catastrophic result. And the moral at the end constitutes the strength of the *ewo*. This is how *ewo* comes to carry the idea of "It is not done, no one does it". The forbidden thing causes death; however, "that which causes death is forbidden" is a notion which precedes "that which is forbidden causes death".

[11] E. G. Parrinder: *West African Religion*, pp. 201 ff.

To sin, again, is to do that which is rotten (*aṣebajẹ*). It also means to do that which is deadly (*aṣeburuku*), chaotic, or absolute perversity. *Iwa buruku* is that which is in absolute conflict with itself or with the norm, that which causes a chaos. On the whole, then, the nature of *ẹse* is determined by the outward results it produces. Sin is that which produces evil as its consequence. This is a pragmatic view in accord with the functional conception of religion which has been indicated previously.

The question which concerns us here does not require a consideration of what specific acts are considered as *ẹsẹ*, neither does it raise the question of that which constitutes the origin or cause of sin. What needs to be pointed out in the present context is that our evidence shows that the African preoccupation with *ẹsẹ*-notion concerns primarily sinfulness rather than sins, the fact of sin in itself rather than isolated acts of sin. African ethnic religion deals with the fact of sinfulness and the effect it produces. The concept of the "forgiveness of sins" (plural, as in the Apostles' Creed) is generally treated as concerned with sinfulness rather than sins, and here it finds a ready understanding in African ethnic theology.

A Christian doctrine of sin close to the heart of African ontological morality will begin with a definite recognition of sin as fundamentally an inward problem of character. The cause of sin will be seen as lying at the centre of human personality, springing out of man's urge for vital force, consisting of the inner motives animating the search for life-force and the extent to which one is able to universalize this desire for life-force. In this context, Christian moral judgement will therefore not be so much judgement of a man's actions as of the person himself, his inner motives, the inner urges of his actions, his standing before God, and the total orientation of his self (life-force) to the self, will and purpose of God.

The condemnation of hypocrisy by our Lord as being the most symptomatic and most virulent of sins is easily understandable if sin and goodness are seen as descriptions of the basic structure of personality. The "inordinate self-love" or pride, which medieval Fathers condemned as the fundamental sin of man, becomes in truth the archetypal expression of sinfulness if morality and sin are taken as concerning the will, motive and attitude. The rejection of a legalistic system of ethics which we find in the New Testament, and which becomes the context for the doctrine of justification by grace through faith, becomes especially significant in an ethical system which lays emphasis on the person and his inner character, his motives, his moral growth and the fitness of his action for a cosmic end of life.

Let us combine the two concepts of sin as based in the person, rooted in personal ontology, with that of sin as an act which becomes the cause of deadly happening to such an extent that the act itself is thereby regarded as absolute perversity. Immediately this is done, the perpetrator of the act himself becomes involved in deadliness, for he has by the act identified himself with the evil. This is the complex situation religion has to deal with. It is the problem of how to extricate an author of evil from the dire consequences of his act, how to restore order in the cosmos, how to reform the sinner's own head, stomach, heart, body, indeed his total personality, and make him new, or a new creature, to use New Testament language.

The question then arises, how does pagan religion deal with this situation of *ese*? It is through the utilization of mythological rites, by re-enacting the sacred history of what happened long ago. Restoration of order, both in the cosmos and in the sinner's own being, is effected only by *what God has done*, or what the gods have done. And that restoration becomes real in experience only as one becomes a participant in that divine event. The *idea* of "forgiveness of sins", letting the prisoner go, might evoke from the pagan the question, "Do you mean that there is nothing to be done?" He would not be referring to what man has to do of his own initiative; his meaning would be, "Is there nothing which God has done which has to be re-enacted so that the sinner may not only feel new but also *become* new?" The Yoruba word for forgiveness is a graphic and pictorial one, *iforiji*. It comes from the myth of the original man prostrating himself before Olodumare and being let free to get up and depart "with his head still on his neck". Forgiveness is letting a sinner get away with his head on when it could have been cut off because of his sin. But this act of the gods becomes real in the experience of an individual sinner as he goes through the ceremony of "washing the head", with the story of the original primordial event being repeated upon his head. The story in oracular form is called *ayajo*, which is literally "the correspond-ing day". As the priest recites the story of "the corresponding day" (*in illo tempore*), the sinner washes his head, beating it with passion and grief and wishing himself well with confes-sion of the past. Forgiveness, in Yoruba religious thought, is more than forgetting the past; it is the giving of a "head", the making of a new creation.

Bishop Neill has suggested that the final test of a non-Chris-tian religion lies in the question, "How does this religion con-ceive of forgiveness of sin and what provision is made for it?" If we accept the validity of this suggestion, a problem arises when we discover that the conception of sin in ethnic religion is different from that in Western thought which we have inherited, and therefore what we offer as a solution may even appear on the premise of ethnic religion to be naïve, inadequate, or blas-phemous. At least, our brief survey of the Yoruba understand-ing of sin indicates that it is possible for the pagan to borrow the words of Anselm's famous answer to Boso in his *Cur Deus Homo*: "Have you not yet considered of what great gravity is sin?"—a peril that has happened, to which one exposes one-self, a tragedy that has been set in motion in the sinner and in the cosmos itself?

"This", writes Dr. Parrinder, "would explain also the apparent unintelligence which the African considers the Euro-pean to display towards native beliefs. 'White people cannot understand', so I have been told, 'things that Africans know'."[12] In other words, is it any wonder that when the Gospel of Christ's work "for us and for our salvation" was proclaimed in terms of the Early Church's explanation of it as a ransom paid to the devil, or in the categories of the code of honour in medieval German feudalistic society whereby Christ is made to pay on the Cross the *wergild* due from man to God for the injury done to his honour by our sinfulness (the whole "special emphases of Moravian and Anglican Evangelical theology"),[13] what the Buganda discovered and rejoiced in was knowledge of the transcendent God who alone is able to *make to happen*, by His act, the cosmic event which is sufficient to redeem man

[12] E. G. Parrinder, *West African Psychology*, p. 12.
[13] J. V. Taylor, *The Growth of the Church in Buganda*, London, S.C.M. Press, 1958, p. 252.

from the *curse* of his sin, participation in which event will make men new creatures, enabled to begin to live life anew? This is what they have been waiting for. And this *is* what Christ has done uniquely, absolutely and finally through the Cross.

7

VITAL PARTICIPATION

The Cohesive Principle of the Bantu Community

Introduction

IN THIS STUDY we shall draw on ideas contained in our recently published work entitled *Un visage africain du christianisme—L'union vitale bantu face à l'unité vitale ecclésiale*, Paris, 1965, pp. 115–146).[1]

On the basis of a study of three Bantu peoples, the Bashi of central Kivu in the Congo, the Rwanda and the Barundi, we reached the conclusion that participation in a common life is the main if not the only basis of all their family, social, political and religious institutions and customs. This life is not static: it can increase or decrease; it is lived in the communion of its members, who can exercise vital influence on one another; it can be touched and handled.

For the sake of clarity, we shall divide the present study into three sections:

1. Unity of life as the centre of cohesion and solidarity among the Bantu.

2. A life which can increase, decrease and interact.

3. The place of the symbol in vital participation.[2]

---

[1] This book includes a summary in English.

[2] As we have extended the area of our research to other Bantu groups in the Congo, we have so far found no difficulty in applying to them the conclusions of our study of the Bashi, the Rwanda and the Barundi. For example, participation or vital union is also the key to the customs of the Bakongo, the Baluba, the Babira, etc. By another method, Father P. Tempels had also reached the same conclusion, in his well-known thesis on vital forces. Although we find this philosophically unsound, it may be justified from a phenomenological standpoint.

I. UNITY OF LIFE

By unity of life or vital union, we mean:

a. A relationship of being and life between each individual and his descendants, his family, his brothers and sisters in the clan, his antecedents, and also with God, the ultimate source of all life.[3]

b. An analogical ontic relationship of each individual with his inheritance, the common property of his family or group, together with all it contains or produces, all that lives and grows in it.[4]

One can say that vital union is the vital link which unites vertically and horizontally the living and departed; it is the life-giving principle which is found in them all. It results from a communion or participation in the same reality, the same vital principle, which unites a number of beings with one another.

What is this life? It is a whole life, individual inasmuch as it is received by each being which exists, and communal or collective inasmuch as each being draws from a common source of life.

The common factor which explains the solidarity of clan or tribe is not at all simple. It is not the life of the senses, nor the life of thought. Neither is it life in the multi-coloured diversity we find in newspapers or in the modern novel. It is life in its simplicity, in its essence. It is life as it has been derived and received from the source of "power", as it turns towards power, is seized by it and seizes it. This life is not destroyed by death, although death may subject it to a change of condition. It does not move in a straight line; it is better to compare it with the circumference of a circle.[5] In other words, there is no break between life and death, but continuity between the two.[6]

This life is therefore neither purely bodily nor purely spiritual, but a life of the "whole man". It is the whole of life, the entire being, being in its totality. This totality of being

---

[3] The Bashi call him *Nyamuzinda* (he who is at the end of everything); the Rwanda and the Burundi, *Imana* (source of all good and all happiness).

[4] Cp. P. Tempels, *op. cit.*, pp. 68–69.

[5] Cp. van der Leeuw, *op. cit.*, pp. 191–92.

[6] This conclusion emerges from the religious practices of the Bantu, in particular from the ancestor-cult.

includes all that belongs to it: inheritance, family or group capital, etc. Indeed, for the *Muntu*, the human personality cannot be thought of without its belongings.

Life in this sense, which is the primary concern of the Bantu, is not only empirical but also *super-empirical* life, life beyond the grave, because for the Bantu the two are inseparable and interdependent.[7]

The life of the individual is grasped as it is shared. The member of the tribe, the clan, the family, knows that he does not live to himself, but within the community. He knows that apart from the community he would no longer have the means of existence. In particular, he knows that his life is a participation in his forefathers' life, and that its preservation and strengthening depend continually on them.

For the Bantu, living is existence in community, it is participation in the sacred life (and all life is sacred) of the ancestors; it is an extension of the life of one's forefathers, and a preparation for one's own life to be carried on in one's descendants.

There is a real continuation of family and individual life after death. The dead constitute the invisible part of the family, clan or tribe, and this invisible part is the most important. At all ceremonies of any importance, at birth, marriage, death, burial, investiture, it is the ancestors who preside, and their will is subordinate only to that of the Creator.

The Bantu believe firmly in a vital communion or life-bond which creates solidarity between members of the same family or clan. The fact of having been born in a particular family, clan or tribe plunges us into a specific vital current, "incorporates" us into it, fashions us according to this community, "ontically" modifies our whole being, and turns it in the direction of the community's way of life and behaviour. Thus the family, clan or tribe is a whole, of which each member is only a part. The same blood, the same life which is shared by all, which all receive from the first ancestor, the founder of the clan, runs through the veins of all. Every effort must be directed to the preservation, maintenance, growth and perpetuation of this common

---

[7] The cult of the departed is based on two beliefs: the survival of the individual after death, and a mutual relationship between the living and the dead. No one questions this twofold belief: it is axiomatic.

treasure. The pitiless elimination of everything which hinders this end, and the encouragement at all costs of everything which furthers it: this is the last word in Bantu customs and institutions, wisdom and philosophy.

We have defined vital union, in the first place, as a relationship of being and life which unites all the members of a communion; and secondly, as an ontic analogical relationship which unites these members to all the things which support and adorn life: heritage and family capital. A second factor must thus be taken into consideration: all that belongs to the ancestors is bound up with their being; objects which belonged to the ancestors (a lance, a drum, a diadem, etc.) may be called the *instruments of vital union*. The Bantu view of life may therefore be seen in two ways:

as a community of *blood*: this is the main primary factor;
as a community of *property*: this is the concomitant factor which makes life possible.

In the light of all this, vital participation among the Bantu may be summarized as follows:

(1) That in which one participates, but which itself participates in nothing (*le Participable imparticipé*): among the Bashi, *Nyamuzinda*, the beginning and the end of all things; among the Rwanda and the Barundi, *Imana*, the source of all happiness. Thus God is thought of as the source of all life and all means of life. "Above all force is God, Spirit and Creator. . . . It is he who has force, power, in himself. He gives existence, power of survival and of increase, to other forces".[8] He is thus the fullness of being and life.

(2) God, willing to transmit his life to other beings, created the first ancestor(s) of the primitive clan(s). The way in which he made them is not described, but it is agreed that the founding ancestor fell down from the sky (*Kigwa:* the Fallen One) and founded the clan.[9] The ancestors were commissioned to hand on and preserve life in their descendants, with the positive intervention of God, who carries on his creative work by the gift of new births. "After him (God) come the first fathers

[8] P. Tempels, op. cit., p. 41.
[9] Cp. H. Tegnaeus, *Le héros civilisateur*, Stockholm, *Studia Ethnographica Upsaliensia*, 1950.

of men, the founders of the different clans. These archpatriarchs were the first to whom God communicated his vital force, with the power of exercising their influence on all their posterity. They constitute the most important link binding men to God. They occupy so exalted a rank in Negro thought that they are not regarded merely as ordinary dead." "They are, after God, the first strengtheners of life, and for each clan they are, as it were, the image, the personification of God."[10]

(3) Beside and even above the disembodied souls of the ancestors, there are the spirits of the old heroes, such as Lyangombe,[11] who are also commissioned by God to strengthen and influence human life. Their cult, a recent one according to the testimony of the older generation, shows the concept of vital union in all its strength.

(4) In this world, man's life is fulfilled inasmuch as it resembles the life of God, the ancestors and the other higher spirits. This resemblance, this vital participation is also the basis of one's rank in society. Social rank is linked with and depends on vital rank, which in turn derives from the influence which departed forefathers exert on the generation of the living. The first ancestor lives on in those who come after him. On the family level, it is the father who carries on the life of the ancestors; on the level of the clan, it is the *patriarch* or chief of the clan; on the level of the tribe or nation, it is the *mwami* (king, big chief) with his mother: he is the mediator and channel of all life and all the means of life. The *mwami* is invested by the representatives of the first founders of the clans and the first occupiers of the land. In this way he becomes the representative, not only of his own ancestors, but of all the ancestors. Since his authority is an extension of patriarchal authority, the king is for the whole tribe or nation what the patriarch is for his family, and the chief of the senior branch for the whole clan.

(5) The name *abaguma* among the Bashi, *abamwe* among the Rwanda and the Barundi—the *one*—is given in the strict sense to all, living or dead, who descend from the same eponymous ancestor, all in whom the same life, the same blood circulate

---

[10] P. Tempels, *op. cit.*, pp. 41–2, 101.
[11] The greatest of the heroes venerated in Rwanda, Burundi, Kivu (Congo), Bunyoro, etc.

in the paternal line; hence, all members of the same family or clan.

(6) By marriage, each of the contracting parties, with all his *baguma* or *bamwe*, enters the family of the other party. Marriage is a bond between two families, who thereby become co-families. Those united in this way by marriage are identified with the *baguma* or *bamwe*.

(7) Blood brothers are also included in the category of *baguma* or *bamwe*. This union, like that of marriage, gathers into itself all the *baguma* or *bamwe* of the contracting parties. The fact of drinking one another's blood has, for those who undergo this rite, the effect of communion in the same life.

(8) Roots in the same soil, the use of the same means of life, subjection to the same authority, produce a similar result to the *buguma* (*cinyabuguma*) or *bumwe*:[12] not a merely legal, political or social result, but one which influences being (*ntu*) itself, and modifies it intrinsically.

The whole of society, the family, the clan, the tribe, the nation, can thus be considered from the point of view of participation. It is even the degree of vital participation which determines the hierarchy of beings and social rank. The *Muntu's* value, in his own eyes and in those of society, is measured by the extent to which he shares in life and hands it on. There is logic in this point of view: the one who gives life or a means of life is superior to the one to whom he gives it.

For the sake of brevity, let us list the hierarchy of beings according to their vital rank and their organic union with one another:

The invisible world:

(1) The source of life, God.
(2) The first participants: the founders of the clans.
   (a) dynastic clans;
   (b) non-dynastic clans.
(3) The spirits of the old heroes. (According to the elder generation, this is a recent cult not found everywhere.)
(4) The disembodied spirits of departed relatives and members of the clan.

---

[12] The Bashi *buguma* or *cinyabuguma*, and the Rwanda and Barundi *bumwe* are exact equivalents of "unity of life" or "vital union".

142

The visible world:

(1) The king or *mwami* and the queen mother; those who share in the royal power and extend it.

(2) Heads of clans, the patriarchs of the senior branch of each clan.

(3) Heads of families. (The father is the centre of family life.)

(4) The members of different families and clans form a single community through the fact of belonging to the same king.

(N.B. Animals, plants, inorganic beings are considered as the extensions and means of life of those to whom they belong. The cosmos, of which man, the *Muntu*, is king, is man's servant, at least in so far as he can draw from it an increase of his being.)

The key to an understanding of Bantu customs and institutions would thus appear to be the fact of community, unity of life. The handing-on of this life, the sharing in this one life, is the first link which unites members of the community. The fact of contributing to its transmission, sharing, preservation or extension is the second element in vital union. All authority has its *raison d'être* in these two elements. He who has given life to another is vitally superior to him; he who is nearer to the source of life, in a given line of descent, has also social precedence; he who procures for his neighbour a means of life, a plot of ground, for example, or a cow, becomes *ceteris paribus* his superior.

Everything is thus explained by participation in life. The closer the point at which one participates is to the source, the higher one's status. The *Muntu's* primary concern is never to interrupt this vital circuit, to give it an ever wider and intenser "magnetic field", to remain united with the first sources and the first channels of life.

Let us crystallize what we have already said.

(1) There is a participation, an intimate ontic relationship, between living and dead members of a family, clan or tribe. The link between them comes from the unity of blood, the common life which circulates in the veins of all the members.

(2) There is an analogous participation between an individual or group and *its* belongings. Thus the hair, the shadow, etc., are extensions of the human being; the inheritance, the group capital, all possessions are vitally bound up with their owner. This is why roots in the same soil, the fact of belonging

to the same master and sharing in the same means of existence, create a vital link of solidarity.

One is therefore justified in speaking of individual participation, i.e. participation between an individual and the extensions of his being, and collective participation, i.e. participation between a group and the extension of its being;[13] in the same way, one can distinguish between vital participation based on community of life, and property participation based on community of means of life.

This first participation, this first element in vital union, namely participation based on community of life, is the basis of the second participation, the link which binds one to the earth, the economic "substratum" or heritage. "The group, like the individual, is not made up only of flesh and blood; it is a complete and self-sufficient whole, animated by a diffused life. The beings of which it is composed are not all visible; around animals and men there move the geniuses of the ground, the forces of vegetation, the spirits of the dead. The bond between them is that of participation. The special function of religion is to recognize, classify and propitiate them. The progress of ideas consists in differentiating them and placing them in a hierarchical order."[14]

Community based on common means of existence is thus included in the community based on sharing in a common life. "In studying these forms of participation between objects or beings and their belongings, we conclude that they are not based on perceived relationships, even such an obvious one as that between a part and the whole, but on a feeling of the real presence of the being or object, immediately suggested by something which belongs to it. This feeling needs no other justification than the fact of being felt."[15]

Although the *Muntu* recognizes the causal nexus in the interplay of ontic influences of being on one another, his world with its causal relationships remains dynamic and fluid. The action of beings on one another is not limited by time and space. On the one hand, the First Cause may transcend these condi-

[13] Cp. J. Przyluski, *La Participation*, Paris, Presses Universitaires de France, 1940, pp. 84–88.
[14] *Ibid.*, p. 120.
[15] L. Lévy-Bruhl, *Carnets*, Paris, Presses Universitaires de France, 1949, p. 206.

tions and allow his subordinates to act independently of them; and on the other hand, since the vital, ontic link between beings in the same community is present and identical in them all, the action and influence of beings on one another meets with no resistance. The causal nexus, independent of conditions in the world, of time and space, is precisely this community, this identity of life and of the means of life. Everywhere the agent meets, in the beings on whom he acts, something of himself, and it is this something which makes his influence effective. "One might say: according to this way of thinking, to exist is to participate in a mystic power, essence or reality. . . . The individual cannot distinguish, within himself, between what is his very own and that in which he participates in order to exist."[16]

These considerations lead to the general conclusion that the keystone of Bantu society appears to be a single principle, that of participation. This participation seems to fulfil the function of integrating particular beings, and placing them within the whole plan of the visible and invisible world, so that each reality finds its place and its truth in its connection and relationship with the whole. Participation may help to meet the need for a doctrine more deeply rooted in concrete and universal life, more sensitive to all the experiences of humanity, more responsive to the aspirations of the human soul and of human thought.

Participation is the element of connection, the element which unites different beings as beings, as *substances*, without confusing them. It is the pivot of the relationships between members of the same community, the link which binds together individuals and groups, the ultimate meaning, not only of the unity which is personal to each man, but of that unity in multiplicity, that totality, that concentric and harmonic unity of the visible and invisible worlds.

II. INCREASE, DECREASE AND INTERACTION

If you ask someone how a chief of a community is chosen, the answer you will probably be given is that he becomes chief residually, by the death of the other elders who had pre-

[16] *Ibid.*, pp. 250–51.

cedence over him, because he is the eldest surviving member of the clan, or because he was nominated by his predecessor or by the elders of the clan. But this reply is inadequate, not to say incorrect. "A man . . . becomes chief of the clan . . . by . . . an inner secretion of vital power, raising the *muntu* of the elder to the rank of intermediary and channel of forces between the ancestors on the one hand, and posterity with its heritage on the other hand."[17]

The Bantu think of the chief as undergoing an ontic change, a profound transformation; he enters upon a new mode of being.[18] This new mode of being modifies or adapts the inner being so that it can live and act according to its new situation, that is to say, it can behave like the ancestors and be a worthy extension of their being. The investiture, by which an heir receives his predecessor's possessions, is the rite intended to effect this inner change.

"The King is not a man . . .
He is a man before he is nominated to the throne;
But once appointed, he separates himself from the ordinary nobility,
And obtains a place apart . . ."[19]

Indeed, before his nomination, before his investiture which consecrates and transforms him, the king is a mere mortal, a man like anyone else. When the finger of God and the ancestors comes and designates him to take over the government of his people, there occurs in him, through this very nomination, which is consecrated by the investiture, a total change, a change of *heart*, in the Hebrew sense of the word.

What has happened? All the vital energies, all the currents of his ancestors' blood, all the life which God has placed in them to be carried on and made fruitful, have burst into this mortal man. They have so strengthened his being, his *ntu*, that he has become, so to speak, the synthesis of the ancestors and the living expression of the Supreme Being and his divine bounty.

This is also the case, to a lesser degree, for inferior chiefs

[17] Tempels, *op. cit.*, pp. 67–68.
[18] We shall not go as far as Tempels, who speaks of a modification of essence (*op. cit.*, p. 68).
[19] A, Kagame, *La Poésie dynastique au Rwanda*, Bruxelles, Institut Royal Colonial Belge, 1951, p. 53.

and sub-chiefs, down to chiefs of clans and fathers of families. Succession is always thought of as an ontic change, a strengthening of life, the "handing over" of something from the departed relatives to their successors.

Just as there may be an increase of being, so a being may also suffer a decrease of life. If the king, after his nomination, is no longer a mere man, he becomes a mortal again when the ancestors, represented by their descendants, the people, and taking account only of the people's interests, cease to have confidence in him.

Since vital union is a relationship of being or life with God, the ancestors and their descendants, and a similar ontic relationship with those belongings which make life possible, a decrease of life will be the result of an interruption in the two-way flowing of the vital current.

The life of a departed being would be diminished by cutting off his relationships with the living members of his family or clan. It is in order that these relationships may never be broken that people set such store on survival in their descendants.

The living, for their part, must go on receiving the vital inflow from the ancestors and departed relatives, or their life will wither. Strength, life is the first thing asked for in all prayers addressed to the ancestors, to departed parents, to the spirits of protecting heroes, and in the wishes in which the Supreme Being is mentioned and asked to intervene.

Life is also diminished by all forms of malice; that is why sorcerers are universally detested. In the same way, it is diminished by any violation of another's rights. Any spiritual or material damage has repercussions on life, and influences it.

The prime evil, the greatest injustice, is to disregard someone's vital rank. This happens "when a junior decides something for himself, disposes of clan property without recognizing elders".[20]

In the same way as "every good office, every help and assistance count before all else as a support, an increase of life to him who is the beneficiary", and "their value is measured directly in terms of this reinforced life", "so every attempt, however insignificant, . . . even against material possessions,

[20] Tempels, op. cit., p. 93.

147

will be considered as an injury to the integrity of his being, the intensity of his life. Every injustice is in the first place an attempt upon the life (i.e. upon the vital force) of the person injured, and the malice in it proceeds from the great respect due to human life, the supreme gift of God. . . . It is therefore not the importance in economic terms of the loss suffered, but the measure of the outrage on life endured, which will serve as the basis of assessment of compensation or damages."[21]

"From the child to the God–Man, solitude excites dread in us all: for we possess power and life only in the community. It is this primeval dread, and no mere trivial fear, that created gods. Dread leads to God, or the devil. . . . But unless we were beings who possessed life only within the community, we should know neither dread nor loneliness."[22]

For the Bantu, beings maintain an intimate ontic relationship with one another, and the idea of distinct beings, side by side, completely independent of one another, is foreign to their thought. "For the Bantu there is interaction of being with being, that is to say, of force with force;[23] transcending the mechanical, chemical and psychological interactions, they see a relationship of forces which we should call ontological. In the created force (a contingent being) the Bantu sees a causal action emanating from the very nature of that created force and influencing other forces."[24]

Every manifestation of Bantu life reflects this interaction of beings on one another. The living strengthen their dead by offerings and sacrifices, and the departed in turn are thought to exert a real vital influence on the living and on their destiny. An indissoluble link, based on participation in the same undivided life, unites this world to the invisible world, and *vice versa*.

In this world, the son, even when he has grown up, "remains always for the Bantu a man, a force, in causal dependence and ontological subordination to the forces which are his father and mother. The older force always dominates the younger. It continues to exercise its living influence over it. . . . The world

---

[21] *Ibid.*, p. 93.
[22] van der Leeuw, *op. cit.*, p. 242.
[23] We do not agree that being and force are identical and interchangeable.
[24] Tempels, *op. cit.*, p. 40.

of forces is held like a spider's web of which no single thread can be caused to vibrate without shaking the whole network." This causality "flows out of the very nature of a created being".[25]

The visible world is one with the invisible; there is no break between the two, still less between their inhabitants, since the family, the clan, the tribe and the nation are thought to extend beyond death, and thus form the invisible and most important element in the community. This community (family, clan, tribe, state) is the sum total of all its members, both living and departed. It would be unthinkable for the living to exist in isolation from the vital influence of the ancestors, just as the existence of the child cannot be considered apart from the influence of its progenitors. Those who have the greatest vital power have the duty and ability to strengthen those who are weaker, and the weaker owe respect to the more powerful, and must turn to them.

Thus the Bantu community is a vital circuit in which members live in dependence on one another, and for one another's good. To leave this circuit, to withdraw from the vital influence of the vitally superior members, would be to be tired of life!

Life and being are thus thought of among the Bantu as a participation in the life, in the being of the ancestors; this explains their sense of solidarity. This life may be handed on; it can exert or be subject to vital influences; it can be increased and diminished; it is the subject matter of Bantu science and philosophy.

In practical life, the Bantu's every effort goes to maintaining solidarity between the members of the community, improving the communication and circulation of life, increasing vital force and preventing the diminution of life.

(1) The ancestor-cult binds the living to the dead and *vice versa*. Its purpose is also to strengthen the being's vitality, and to prevent its decline.

(2) The hero-cult serves to increase and strengthen vital energies. It is even an attempt to rise above life; it is an aspiration to a higher life which will place the initiate above the ordinary level.

[25] *Ibid.*, pp. 40–41.

(3) The science and practice of diviners, healers and sorcerers aims at capturing and using the interaction of natural forces which God has created and put at men's disposal.

(4) The social order is founded on vital union, the growth of the inner self and the interdependence of vital influence. Ethics and law follow logically from the conception of beings and their ontic connection.[26] "Every customary law worthy of the name (and which is really law; not a toleration of abuse) is inspired and justified, from the Bantu point of view, by the philosophy of vital force, of the increase, interdependence, influence and hierarchy" of life. "Ethics on the one hand . . . and law on the other . . . are founded for the Bantu on the same basic principles, and constitute an organic whole."[27]

The social order is based on the ontological order. Every organization, political or other, which offends this principle could not be recognized by the Bantu as orderly or normal.[28]

Everything which is called "tabu", all prohibitions and bans, find their explanation in this bond of solidarity which unites members of a community with one another in a common concern that this bond should be maintained, in the belief in the increase and decrease of life and the interaction and interdependence of beings and vital forces.

III. THE ROLE OF THE SYMBOL IN VITAL PARTICIPATION

If the bond uniting the members of a Bantu community is simply that of participation, "that is to say, a solidarity in fact, showing itself in two inseparable ways, one personal, the other real",[29] the main and often only means which members have of entering into contact with one another and strengthening their union is the symbol.

In the etymological sense, the word symbol (*symbolon*) is a sign of recognition. At first it was an object cut in two, the two parts being kept by two people who had exchanged hospitality. They handed them on to their children, and when the two halves were put together, the bearers could be recognized,

[26] Cp.Tempels, *op. cit.*, pp. 78–80, 85–89, 93, 94, 96, 97, 100, 101, 106, 107.
[27] E. Possoz, *Eléments de droit coutumier nègre*, Elisabethville, 1942, p. 30.
[28] Cp. Tempels, *op. cit.*, pp. 79–80.
[29] Przyluski, *op. cit.*, p. 148.

and the former relationship of hospitality proved.[30] Later, the symbol became a sign of recognition by which people who had been separated for a long time could make themselves known to one another; in particular, it was an object by which parents could recognize in later life the children they had abandoned;[31] hence, any sign, token, stamp, badge, password, etc.[32]

In the real sense, "symbol" means "that which represents something else because of an analogical correspondence. It is used:

(1) of the factors in a strict algorism: numerical, algebraic symbols:
(2) of any sign which evokes (by a natural relationship) something which is absent or invisible: the sceptre is the symbol of kingship."[33]

In order to understand the importance of symbols for the Bantu, one must remember:

a. the distinction they make between the outward appearance of a visible being, and the being itself, which is an invisible force. "But the inner, invisible force can concentrate or manifest itself more particularly in one part of the visible being. The vital force can be intensified and compacted; it can exteriorise itself at what we may call a nodal point or vital centre."[34]

This vital centre, this "sign" or symbol of an invisible power, is the main element, the active principle, the source of energy. All cures, all talismans and amulets, etc., contain some of this vital energy. People procure the *vital knot* of more powerful beings in order to increase their own strength. This is what hunters do for themselves and their dogs, since hunting is a life-struggle between the hunter and the game: they equip themselves with forces which can overcome those of the game.

b. the existence of certain laws or principles which enable one to recognize these vital knots in certain beings.

[30] A. Bailly, *Dictionnaire grec-français*, Paris, Larousse, 1895, s.v. *symbolon.*
[31] *Ibid.*
[32] Lalande, *Vocabulaire technique et critique de la philosophie*, Paris, Presses Universitaires de France, 1960, s.v. *symbole.*
[33] *Ibid.*, section A.   [34] Tempels, *op. cit.*, p. 53.

(1) The first of these laws is the well-known *similia similibus curantur*. "Ethnologists explain this by declaring that a force acts by likeness and by agreement." Nevertheless "this likeness cannot be the causal foundation of vital influence. But the resemblance between the murderous force of the lion or of the crocodile and the intentions which actuate the hunter or the fisherman lead the Bantu to believe that the forces of these great carnivores can be used in the exercise of the trade of hunter or fisherman; or rather in the struggle in which they engage respectively against the prey and the fish. The resemblance is not the active agent, but only the proof or sign of a particular force."[35]

(2) "Another law says that the living being exercises a vital influence on everything that is subordinate to him and on all that belongs to him. . . . The fact that a thing has belonged to anyone, that it has been in strict relationship with a person, leads the Bantu to conclude that this thing shares the vital influence of its owner", since it forms part of his life.[36] It is not a matter, as anthropologists put it, of contact or sympathetic magic. "It is neither contact nor 'sympathy' that are the active elements, but solely the vital force of the owner, which acts, as one knows, because it persists in the being of the thing possessed or used by him."[37]

(3) A third law allows one to recognize, in certain cases, vital forces or intentions. "A living man's word and gesture are considered, more than any other manifestation, to be the formal expression or sign of his vital influence. From that, if words or gestures produce favourable or unfavourable effects on someone, one may conclude that someone else is exercising his vital influence, for good or ill, upon him. What one is in the habit of calling 'magic of expressed wish' or 'magic of mimicry', or 'imitative magic', indicates this kind of exercises; but here again, there are neither words nor mimicry that exercise a power, but only signs that externalise the action of the vital influence and make it known to third parties."[38]

Let us gather, from the customs and institutions of the Bashi, the Rwanda and the Barundi, a few facts which reveal the *Muntu's* tendency towards symbolism:

[35] Tempels, *op. cit.*, p. 54.
[37] *Ibid.*, p. 54.
[36] Tempels, *op. cit.*, p. 54.
[38] *Ibid.*, pp. 54–55.

(1) Among the Bashi, the child who is born feet first brings on his parents a tabu called *kashindi*. There is also a whole series of prohibitions which apply to a pregnant woman.

(2) Among the names given to new-born babies, there are some which are intended to repel death or misfortune. These names are derived from animals or repulsive materials. Similarly, some are intended to attract the favourable influence of a powerful person.

(3) All the ceremonial surrounding the birth of twins can be explained only in the light of symbolism. Why must the twins be of the same sex, so as not to attract misfortune? Why must they both be punished when only one is guilty? Why, if one has died and his brother is to be beaten, must one beat something else in place of the one who has died?

(4) Before a daughter is given in marriage, she must go and sacrifice under the very tree (*mulinzi*) which was the altar at which she was initiated into the cult of the hero *Lyangombe*. During the sacrifice, which is made at the mother's or fiancée's house, and which is the decisive rite in which the girl's family gives or refuses to give her in marriage, the father watches a pot of banana juice fermenting. If the liquid flows on to the side where the children are sleeping, it is a sign of blessed fertility; if it flows on to the opposite side, it is a sign of sterility.

(5) As the father lets his daughter go, he blesses her by ejecting over her face and chest a mouthful of banana juice. The sprinkling of lustral water by the future father-in-law expresses his greeting to his daughter-in-law. A fiancé greets his wife-to-be by spitting a mouthful of milk over her face as a symbol of her future motherhood.

(6) All the marriage ceremonies are full of symbolism: the river-jump among the Bashi, the changing of the bride's name, her instruction, etc. Even the additional formalities are significant: the lesson in filial piety, consisting in an offering of food to the parents, the communion meal, the genuflexion which the bridegroom goes to make at the crossroads, etc. The bride-wealth and the covenant token are the symbol of the vital bond uniting the two families, especially the token, which is also intended to symbolize the daughter in her own family. Just as in the bridegroom's family the bride acts as a link connecting the two families, so in the bride's family the token is

meant to perpetuate and symbolize her presence, and to be a unifying factor between the two families.

(7) What is commonly called *totem* means for the Bantu simply the symbol, emblem or sign of those who descend from the same eponymous ancestor. It may be described as a sign of recognition and of clan solidarity.

(8) Services rendered to the dead are marked by striking symbolism: rubbing with butter or cow-dung, the placing of a few seeds in the corpse's hands, the torch (lit or unlit according to whether the departed has offspring or not), which precedes the funeral cortège; the hand-washing on the tomb and the breaking of a pot; the wife accused of hastening her husband's death, who bestrides the tomb to prove her innocence; the prohibitions characteristic of mourning; the purifications marking its end; the funeral meal given by the family of the departed, etc.

(9) The *mwami* or king is a representative, a bearer of power, a "hand used by power".

The diadem belonging to the *mwami* of the Bashi contains part of his predecessor's body, and realistically symbolizes his union with his ancestors. This insignia never left the sovereign's head. The other objects which had belonged to the royal ancestors, like the *Kalinga* drum of the monarch of the Rwanda, and its brother *Karyenda* belonging to the Burundi monarch, are also links between the holder of power and his ancestors. The mysterious seeds which the heir is supposed to bring as signs of his predestination; among the Bashi, the beautiful ceremonies of royal investiture and its annual renewal (*omubande*); those of the *muganuro* among the Barundi; the public expiations at the court of the *mwami* of the Rwanda, etc., are full of deep significance.

(10) The blood-covenant, practised between the members of different clans, but never between members of the same clan, is meaningless apart from its symbolism. It can be more easily understood if one remembers that the blood-covenant is also practised between the cultic genius, *Lyangombe*, and his devotees. Here, blood itself is symbolized by a liquid which looks like blood.

The blood-covenant can never be added to a natural union, but imitates it, and has the purpose of extending it beyond the limits of the family and the clan. It thus transcends the racial and tribal setting, and opens, up vast possibilities for the expansion and widening of the family. A blood-covenant between the spirit of the hero *Lyangombe* and his neophyte shows the *Muntu's* longing to enter into communion with the suprasensible world, just as the offerings to disincarnate souls show his attempt to remain in communion with invisible realities.

(11) Communion through food only takes place between those who are, or wish to be, on peaceful, friendly or brotherly terms. Eating from the same dish or drinking from the same straw, means entering into interaction with someone else, letting his vital influences be exchanged with one's own. That is why a man under a tabu would contaminate all who ate or drank with him. He must be isolated. Among the Bantu almost all marriage ceremonies, sacrifices to the souls of the ancestors, etc., are concluded by a communion meal. At the investiture of the *mwami* of Gushi, and at the annual renewal ceremony, the *mwami* has a communion meal sent to all the chiefs, sub-chiefs and notables under his jurisdiction; to be deprived of this would be a sign that one was about to fall from power.

The offering to the dead and the blood-covenant appear to be the supreme point of Bantu communion. On its lower levels, this communion of vital participation is found in every exchange of the means of life, every common meal or drink, and every gift; it reaches a paroxysm of realism in the blood-covenant, in which a man really does give himself to his friend; they "drink each other", fusing or putting into a common pool the very principle of life. Further than this one cannot go in communion understood as participation.

(12) All "magic" practices, by which I mean the art and science of healers, sorcerers and diviners, are full of symbols.

(13) In the cult of the disembodied souls of ancestors, and of the great spirit *Lyangombe*, the ancestor or hero is supposed to take possession of the officiating priest. The devotee's inner self is overpowered and transformed, so that the priest believes himself "transpersonalized" and identified with his ancestor, or with the genius of the hero whom he is celebrating—all this through a few phrases and gestures!

(14) Despite its simplicity, or perhaps because of it, the

cult of the Supreme Being is equally revealing. God is the great Transcendent One: unlike the spirits, he does not need to be vitally assisted and strengthened. His life is an inexhaustible source from which beings draw their life. He is generous, he gives of his superfluity without ever exhausting or impoverishing himself; he therefore claims nothing material or tangible in return.

The poverty of the worship of God is a confession of his transcendence, and also of his continual, intimate, immanent presence among and in his creatures.

Whatever aspect of symbolism we consider, it appears to be the effort of the human spirit to make contact with an invisible power, with the spirit world; it seems also to break down the barriers surrounding "man, that fragment in society and in the midst of the Cosmos": it is an effort at unification. Hence the concept of a symbol includes three main elements.

(1) *Something perceived by the senses:* a living being, such as the king, who symbolizes national unity and divine authority; the clan patriarch who symbolizes the ancestors' authority over their descendants; the totem, symbol of the clan's unity, etc.; a word, such as the name of the ancestor, the names of powerful people, animals, substances, etc.; actions and gestures, and so on.

(2) *The hierophantic factor*, the contact with an invisible power, with the sacred. The symbol serves to put one in touch with the instruments, channels or reserves of divine power and the invisible forces, by means of a certain correspondence or resemblance, a relationship of meaning or analogy. There is established, between the being symbolized and the person who comes into contact with him through the symbol, a certain current, an exchange of life and vital energies. In this way, the most elementary activity in life may be made sublime by being uncovered at the point at which it touches the "divine" ("divine" being understood in the sense of anything which has a more than human power of transmitting, increasing or influencing life).

(3) *The unifying and effective element.* The being symbolized is so completely present to and united with its symbol, at least in the operative (as distinct from the ontic) order, that it becomes possible for it to exercise its action and influence as if space

and time did not exist. In this way its action may touch anyone who makes contact with the symbol. The symbolic experience therefore means "not so much I and the world as I in the world". It abolishes the duality between man and the world, and tends towards their unification.[39] All creatures are a gift of the creator to man for maintaining his existence, and to help increase and safeguard his life.

Conclusion

The life-relationship on which, among the Bantu, the unity of communities and individuals is founded, this communication which is a sharing in life and in the means of life, this effort towards ontic growth, self-transcendence and enrichment, find a sublime and transcendent realization in the Church of Christ, which is also a community of life, whose vital principle is a sharing in the life of the Trinity, humanized in the Word of God made Man.

That which was from the beginning, which we have heard, which we have seen with our eyes, which we have looked upon and touched with our hands, concerning the word of life—the life was made manifest, and we saw it, and testify to it, and proclaim to you the eternal life which was with the Father and was made manifest to us—that which we have seen and heard we proclaim also to you, so that you may have fellowship with us; and our fellowship is with the Father and with his Son Jesus Christ" (1 John 1: 1–3 RSV).

This participation is never complete in this life, but it tends to become more and more intense through likeness to the Son of God, the Founder of the Church, the "clan" which came down from heaven.

We are convinced that the Bantu principle of vital participation can become the basis of a specifically African theological structure. We shall need much patience, common sense and prudence, but also courage, to construct such a theology.

Communion as participation in the same life and the same means of life will, we believe, be the centre of this ecclesiological theology. Symbolism, which makes this communion-in-parti-

[9] Cf. C. Zucker, *Psychologie de la superstition*, Paris, Payot, 1952, pp. 44–45.

cipation perceptible and tangible; and sacramentalism, its culmination, which extends and perpetuates the Holy Humanity of the Word, this instrument joined with Divinity: these will be the effective means by which this theology may be realized and shown forth.

8

ESCHATOLOGY*

IT IS OUR intention to discuss this subject in three parts. In the first, we shall consider African eschatological ideas; in the second, our attention will be centred on Christian ideas on the subject. Finally, we shall attempt a correlation of African and Christian ideas.

I. AFRICAN ESCHATOLOGY

1 *Time*

In traditional thought, Africans are not concerned with the academic questions of Time. For them, Time is a composition of events which have been realized, those which are occurring simultaneously or which are immediately to occur. What has not been realized belongs in reality to *No-Time*. It might one day, however, become Time, i.e. become realized, actualized, or be "born" into the realm of Time (composition of events).

(i) *"Past" and "Present"*

The linear concept of Time, with a Past, Present and Future, stretching from infinity to infinity, is foreign to African thinking, in which the dominant factor is a virtual absence of the Future. By our definition Time is a composition of events, and since the Future events have not occurred, the Future as a necessary linear component of Time is virtually absent. Such is either *potential Time*, with certainty of its eventual realization, or *No-Time*, lying beyond the conceptual horizon of the people. The Future has no independent existence of its own, since the events that compose Time have not occurred in it, and once they occur

---

* Cp. J. S. Mbiti, "African Concept of Time", *African Theological Journal* (Mukumira, Tanzania), No. 1, February 1968; pp. 8–20. [Ed.]

it is no longer Future but the Present and the Past. To Africans, Time has to be experienced to make sense. Therefore the essence of Time is what is Present and what is Past. Time moves backwards rather than forwards, from the Now (Present) to the Past. These two dimensions are the dominant Periods in the life of the individual, the community, the nation and humanity at large.

To avoid the thought associations with the English words *Past* and *Present*, I propose to use the Swahili terms *Zamani* and *Sasa*, to cover these two periods respectively. The two Time-periods overlap, without a clear-cut or necessary separation between them. *Sasa* is not just a point of NOW in Time. It is the period in which people exist, and within which they project themselves primarily into the past, and to a less extent into the future. The *Sasa* is a Time-period with a future, present and past, and it might rightly be called the *Micro-Time*.[1] But what is future in the *Micro-Time* is something so real, so certain that it is almost actualized and has nearly passed away. When people live in this kind of future, they have virtually experienced it. But if the future in the *Sasa*-period is remote, say some years hence, then it is hardly thought or spoken of, and has little or no impact upon the people. Furthermore, research into a number of East African languages[2] has shown that these languages do not possess a vocabulary which can directly express concepts of a distant future, and if one makes a circumlocutory attempt to describe something in the distant future, the expression becomes vague or conveys little meaning, if anything. Events in the *Sasa* must be about to occur, in the process of actualization, or they must have been recently actualized or experienced. The individual, alone or with the community, experiences the *Sasa* period; he participates in it, and only in so doing can it become meaningful to him. To speak of something yet to be is really to project oneself into that phenomenon, and to be a participant in it, witness it, or simply be contemporaneous with it. The *Sasa* period is not mathematically constant, and different people have different quantities and qualities of *Sasa*. Individual *Sasa* is constantly changing but never ending.

[1] From *mikros* (Greek)—small, little (of time); cp. *makros*—long.
[2] Kikamba, Gikuyu, Luganda, among others.

The *Zamani* period, on the other hand, might be called *Macro-Time*. It has its own past, present and future, and overlaps with or intrudes into the *Sasa* period. Before events are incorporated into the *Zamani*, they have to become actualized in the *Sasa*. Then they move "backwards" into the *Zamani* period, in which everything finds its termination, its halting point. It is the storehouse for all phenomena and events, a vast ocean of Time where everything gets absorbed into an aspect of reality which is neither after nor before. Like *Sasa*, *Zamani* has both quantity and quality: it can be good, long, short, bad, etc., in relation to a particular phenomenon; and likewise, *Zamani* cannot be described mathematically.

It is to be noted that Time and Space are closely connected in African life and thought, but it is unnecessary to enter into this discussion here.

(ii) *Time Reckoning and Chronology*

When Africans reckon Time chronologically, it is for a concrete and specific purpose. Numerical calendars are, to our knowledge, non-existent in traditional society.[3] What we do find might be called "phenomenon-calendars", in which events are considered in relation to one another and as they take place in Time (i.e. as they constitute Time); Time is not reckoned for its own sake. The day, the month, the year, one's life-span, the history of the nation (tribe) are all divided up according to particular key events. Divisions of the day would be reckoned according to commonly accepted or acknowledged events, e.g. sunrise, milking-time, working in the fields, driving cattle back to the villages, cooking the evening meal, etc. It does not matter whether the sun rises at 6 a.m. or 6.30 a.m., nor does it matter whether the evening meal is prepared from 7 p.m. or 8 p.m. It is the event—the content of Time—which matters more than the exact mathematics of Time. Lunar months, rather than numerical "calendar" months, have names according to the main events or the meteorological features of the Time, e.g. the hot month, the month of the first rains, the weeding month, the beans harvest month, the hunting month, etc. It does not matter whether the hunt-

---

[3] If one does find numerical calendars, they are likely to be of short duration, stretching perhaps to a few decades, but certainly not into the realm of centuries.

ing month lasts 25 or 35 days; the emphasis is on the phenomena.

The year is likewise composed of events, but of a generally wider nature. Where the community is agricultural, seasonal activities may compose an agricultural calendar. The actual number of days, be that 300 or 380, does not matter; a year is a complete year when all its component seasons and activities are realized in full. Since years differ mathematically, but not event-wise, numerical calendars are meaningless, if not "impossible", and it is no wonder that they either do not exist or do not extend beyond a few decades. Outside the reckoning of the year, the African Time concept is silent and indifferent. People expect the years to come and go, in an endless rhythm like that of day and night, and the waxing and waning of the moon.

2 *History*

African peoples have their national histories, but for them history moves "backwards" from the *Sasa* period to the *Zamani*. There is no concept of history moving forwards to a future climax, or to a better future, or to an end of the world.[4] The future does not dominate African thinking, and they do not therefore expect it to usher in a "Golden Age". There is neither "The End" nor a "belief in progress" (i.e. the development of human activities and achievements from a low to a higher degree). The centre of gravity for human thought and activities is the *Zamani* rather than the virtually non-existent or myopic future.

The pre-history is, in African thought, dominated by the Myth. There are innumerable myths all over the continent, explaining the creation, the first man, the "fall" of man, the coming of death, the separation of heaven (sky) and earth, the origin of the nation and its arrival in its present area, etc. Such history is often telescoped into a very compact oral tradition. If we attempt to fit such traditions into a mathematical Time-scale, they would cover only a few centuries, although in reality they stretch much further back. Thus, people look to the *Zamani*; for it is not an extinct period but one

---

[4] The only exception I have found is the Sonjo tribe, about which more is said below.

which is full of activity and happenings. God created all things in this period; death came into the world in this period; the ethics, customs and wisdom of the nation emerged in this period; the "Golden Age" for the nation lies in the *Zamani*. It is really a history of origins or genesis, and it forms the foundation for the nation's existence.

Human life follows a rhythm of Nature which nothing can destroy: birth, puberty, initiation, marriage, procreation, old age, death, entry into the company of the departed and eventually into the company of the spirits. Another rhythm is also at work: that of days and nights, months (moons), seasons and years; this also nothing can change. This two-fold rhythm of Nature is "everlasting": as it happened in the past, it is happening now and it will do so for ever. There is no "end" to this continuous rhythm and cycles, and there is no "world to come". People neither worry about the future nor build castles in the air. Time has no end. But certain events are more meaningful than others, e.g. birth, death, marriage, and the like on the individual level; and planting, harvest, epidemics, etc., on the community or national level. If there is an unusual event, such as an eclipse of the sun or moon, or drought or the birth of twins, this would be considered a bad omen or an event requiring attention. Such moments are given more attention than others and may often be marked by religious rites.

In the African understanding of history, man looks back from whence he came, and man is certain that nothing shall bring this world to a conclusion. Therefore, there are no myths of the *Endzeit*,[5] whereas the *Urzeit*[6] is full of them. In our extensive research in this field we have come across only one people, the Sonjo of Tanzania, which maintains an eschatological and apocalyptic myth about the "end" of the world.

The Sonjo people are small, numbering about 4,500 in 1957. In their eschatological myth it is held that when the end of the world draws near the sun will turn into darkness (evidently from a thick cloud of dust, a swarm of bees and a flock of birds), then two suns will rise (one from the east and the other from the west) and when they meet in the middle the world will end.

[5] I.e. culmination of history.
[6] I.e. primeval age.

At this point Khambageu, the hero-God figure of Sonjo religion, "comes down" to earth and saves the Sonjo people, while the remainder of mankind is probably destroyed. This is the only people that we know of in Africa which has notions of a historical "end" of the world. It is exceptional and does not invalidate our main argument. Exactly how this myth came into being among the Sonjo is unknown, but certainly it is not due to Christian influence in modern times, as far as present scholarly evidence goes.[7]

3 Death and Immortality

Almost all over Africa traditional myths assume that man was originally intended to inherit immortality. Death came only afterwards, caused, it is most commonly held, by man's disobedience, or by the maltreatment or failure of the messenger of immortality. But while death is thus regarded as an unnatural impostor, it did not, however, do away completely with man's immortality. As far as one has been able to find out, the belief in the continuation of life after physical death exists among all African peoples, though certainly with varying degrees of emphasis. The Time factor is the link between the living and the departed, and the relationship between these two groups forms the focal area of activity in most African religions.

Physical death is accepted as both inevitable and unnatural. There are often, if not always, immediate causes, such as witchcraft, and possibly the departed and the spirits; occasionally God himself (or another divinity) may be considered as causing or allowing death as a punishment to the individual. Upon physical death the individual, however, is not annihilated. His body certainly rots behind, but the soul or spirit continues to exist. Man is a composition of both physical and non-physical entities. After the death of the body the non-physical person still lives on. He is *remembered* by relatives and friends who knew him in this life. Thus, he is maintained alive in the *Sasa* period. People continue to recall his words, his personal traits, and in many societies libations are poured and food-

[7] The only serious work done on the Sonjo is by Robert F. Gray, *The Sonjo of Tanganyika*, London, International African Institute for O.U.P., 1963. Our brief summary of Sonjo eschatology is derived from this book. Another piece of work on this particular myth is by H. A. Fosbrooke, "Hambageu, the god of the Wasonjo", *Tanganyika Notes and Records*, Dar-es-Salaam, 1955, No. 35, pp. 38–43.

offerings made to him. If he appears, it is often to his own family, especially to the other members, and he is recognized *by name* as so-and-so. This period may last for up to four or even five generations, so long as someone who knew the departed also dies, then the former departed passes out of the horizon of the *Sasa* period, and in effect he "dies" as far as his family is concerned.

So long as he is remembered by name, he is not really dead: he is alive, and such a person we would call the *living-dead*. The *living-dead* is dead in body but alive in the other world, and in the memory of those who knew him as a person. It is vitally important, therefore, that everyone should have someone to remember him after death. So long as the *living-dead* is remembered, he is experiencing *personal immortality*. This personal immortality is also externalized and realized in the physical continuation of the individual through procreation, some of the progenies bearing the traits of their progenitors.

When with the passing of Time the *living-dead* "die", relative to their immediate families and acquaintances, they do not necessarily vanish out of existence. Now they enter into *collective immortality*—the continuation of life in which they become ordinary spirits rather than formal members of the human families. People may even lose touch with and interest in them altogether. They are now members of the family of spirits, and if they appear to people they are not recognized by name and may cause fear and resentment. Their names may still be mentioned, especially in genealogies, but they are empty names, more or less devoid of a personality, or at best with a mythological personality built around fact and fiction. They have no personal communication with families of their now distant progenies. In some cases, however, they become guardians of the clan or nation, and may be mentioned or appealed to in religious rites of local or national importance. The cult of these spirits and the *living-dead* often eclipses direct worship of God.

4 *The After-Life*

While African peoples acknowledge the continuation of life after death, whatever ideas they have of the "immortality of the soul" are rather mechanical. The soul does not rise to higher spiritual or ethical heights. Life goes on in the next world in practically the same way as it does here; indeed, the next world is a carbon copy of this present life, with perhaps only a few differences. The *living-dead* may, at best in some tribes, act as intermediaries between God and the living; and when libation is poured and offerings made to them or to the spirits, it would generally be acknowledged that God is the ultimate recipient. The departed acquire more "power" (*mana*), which is not, however, a reward, but something that comes to them like old age coming upon everyone.

Among many African peoples, some of the distant real or mythological leaders and heroes of the nation become deified or elevated to the status of demiurges. This seems to be more common among those peoples who have traditional central governments headed by a king or chief. Such kings or chiefs acquire a halo of myths, and a number of them are even assimilated into the nation's cosmology. But for ordinary souls or spirits, life simply continues with almost unbroken "monotony": working in the field, herding cattle, hunting, getting married and raising families, etc. The land of the departed is neither better nor worse than that of the living.

Whether one is later deified or not depends on the living, and there is nothing to hope for or look forward to in the after life. The hereafter is simply an inevitable and unavoidable part of existence. Even where there is a belief in reincarnation, this too is not a hope or reward for the after life, and he who is reincarnated is neither better nor worse off than he who is not. The hereafter is, for African people, devoid of hope or promise. One is simply gathered to one's forefathers, and that is about all. There is no spiritual stature to be acquired: thieves remain thieves, kind people continue to be kind, *ad infinitum*. In some cases the spirits are said to die also, but they may rise again and continue to live.

Beyond these observations, ideas about the after life are seemingly vague and sometimes 'contradictory'. This is a field which requires more research than has hitherto been done.

5 *Judgement*

In the African understanding of the after life, the concept of judgement hardly plays a part; the few known exceptions to this statement will presently be noted. In the hereafter there are no rewards to be coveted, and no punishment to be avoided; there is neither heaven to long for, nor hell to be threatened with. The land of the departed is thought in some societies to be in the underworld; others consider it to be in the uninhabited parts of the wilderness, in rocks, caves or forests; and yet others consider it vaguely to be in the sky "with God". It is rare to find it spoken of in terms of a paradise. Thus, for example, the Bachwa Pygmies living in the Equatorial Province of Congo Kinshasa believe that after death people go to the village of God where all suffering and disease, etc., are abolished, and where there is abundance of comfort, happiness and much game for hunting.'[8] This is, however, the destiny of everyone, and there are no conditions attached to it. Among the Yoruba of Nigeria, it is believed that at death the individual appears before God to give account of his earthly life. The Yoruba thus say,

> All that we do on earth,
> We shall account for kneeling in heaven.

Again,

> We shall state our case at the feet of
> Olodumare.[9]

Among the LoDagaa of Ghana and Upper Volta, it is believed that after death the spirit travels to the land of the departed, and *en route* it must cross a river. If the person led a good life, he is ferried across without difficulties. But if he led an evil life (such as a witch, thief, etc.) he suffers at the river and in the land of the spirits.[10]

Perhaps with increasing knowledge we shall hear of other African societies which have something to say about rewards and punishment in the after life. Even where judgement comes into the picture of the hereafter, it is on the individual; it is not an eschatological judgement on the entire humanity or the

[8] P. Schebesta, *My Pygmy and Negro Hosts*, London, Hutchinson, 1936, p. 236.

[9] E. B. Idowu, *op. cit.*, p. 199. Professor Idowu tells us also that "the Yoruba aged look forward with longing or dread in anticipation of what may be awaiting them in the new life where they are bound to fare according to their deserts" (p. 189).

[10] J. R. Goody, *Death, Property and the Ancestors*, London, Tavistock Publications, 1962, p. 371 ff. There is "punishment" for all, administered by older spirits in the spirit-land, "the Country of God"; but evidently God also helps in carrying out some form of punishment. Everyone is, however, finally "set free" from his doom, after a certain length of time.

universe. Generally it is accepted that God punishes people, and rewards them, in this life. There is nothing awaiting them when they die, for sin is chiefly an offence against one's neighbour (the living or the living-dead) and it is punishable here and now. God's favour is unmerited: He makes some people rich and others poor, He gives healthy bodies to some and weak bodies to others. This is the predestinarian state of affairs, and a man's earthly life has few or no consequences, for better or for worse, in the after life.

Although the way to the after life is a one-way street, the departed may indeed return to visit their relatives and friends; they never return, however, to take up permanent residence in this life. They expect to be remembered through proper burial rites (e.g. among the Nyakyusa of Tanzania), and through offerings, and libations, and to be honoured at the religious rites of their respective "former" families. Apart from folk stories, there is no belief in a resurrection of either the individual or the entire company of the departed. And even where resurrection ideas exist, such resurrection takes place in the *Zamani* period and is not something awaiting the individual in the future. Furthermore, the resurrection does not result in a better or new body. It would seem that, for practical purposes, the place of resurrection beliefs is taken up by a belief in reincarnation. Reincarnation is, however, primarily of personality traits, rather than of the entire person, and when an individual is reborn he does not cease to have his own separate existence any more than a father ceases to exist when his son is born. Again this is a field which requires further research, and one must reserve judgement at this stage.

6 *Conclusions and Consequences of African Eschatology*

A number of significant points seem to emerge from the above:

(1) The concept of "the end of the world" is both absent and meaningless in African traditional life and thought. Everything follows an unending rhythm of Nature: days, months, seasons and years; birth, marriage, procreation, death and entry into the company of the departed.

(2) African languages (at least those which we have examined), lack a future dimension of Time beyond a short dis-

tance of months or years. People neither set their hopes in the future, nor worry about distant impending events. There are no mathematical calendars, but only phenomenon calendars determined by human events and natural phenomena.

(3) Life in the hereafter is a carbon copy of the present; it inspires neither hope nor longing. There is no "Golden Age", no "Paradise", and no "Resurrection", upon which to anchor one's hope. The after life is simply a mechanical, inevitable continuation of life, generally neither better nor worse than life in the present world. There are, generally speaking, neither rewards nor punishment awaiting individuals at death. Punishment and rewards come in this life.

(4) African peoples are extremely sensitive to, and conscious of, the spirit-world, which is believed to be very close to this world, with only a thin veil separating the two. Most religious activities are concentrated on the relationship between these two worlds. The spirit-world is peopled by the *living-dead*, ordinary spirits, and real or mythological founders and leaders of the nation. Some of these beings act as intermediaries between God and man, and some may even be deified.

(5) Great emphasis is laid on the *Zamani* period, the *Macro-Time*. It is the period which forms the foundation of the people's existence: the period of the creation of the world and of man, the birth of the nation, the emergence of national traditions and customs, the period of the "ancestors" and patriarchs. Whereas the *Urzeit* abounds in myths, there are no corresponding eschatological myths of the *Endzeit*. We find, among almost every people of Africa, myths of the coming of death to mankind, but no eschatological myths of the resurrection of mankind; there are myths of the "fall" of man, but no myths of man's "redemption"; there are myths that tell about the separation of heaven (sky) from earth, but no eschatological myths of their conjunction; there are myths of the separation between God and man, but no eschatological myths of their union. Thus, traditional African eschatology is "natural" and lacks a "redemptive" dimension. Man accepts death, separation from God, the gulf between heaven and earth, etc., as natural, inevitable, absolute and immutable. Creation neither grows old, nor is it renewed. God exercises His rule from a transcendental position, being available when needed,

in His immanent aspect. But there are no traditional concepts of the "Kingdom of God", either present or future.

The area of African Eschatology presents points of contact with Christian Eschatology, and the latter would undoubtedly enrich the former. Our understanding of African Eschatology may, in turn, shed some new light on our study of Christian Eschatology. We proceed now to consider, briefly, Christian Eschatology and how it might be linked with African Eschatology.

II. CHRISTIAN ESCHATOLOGY

This is a vast subject, with an enormous amount of literature, and in a short paper like this it is obviously impossible to do justice to it. Some of the familiar names in modern scholarship include J. Weiss, R. H. Charles, A. Schweitzer, E. von Dobschütz, R. Otto, A. F. Loisy, C. H. Dodd, T. W. Manson, C. J. Cadoux, T. F. Glasson, R. Bultmann, O. Cullmann, W. G. Kümmel, J. Jeremias, J. A. T. Robinson, E. Grässer, and many others.

Much of the background to Christian Eschatology is to be found in Jewish Eschatology and Apocalyptic. In particular we mention the Jewish view of history by which history is divided into two: This Age and The Age to Come.[11] One is evil, full of pain and sorrow, the period during which the chosen people are oppressed; the other is to be quite the opposite, full of happiness, and one in which God's reign is fully established. The Age to Come was literally the age to come, as far as Jewish Eschatology was concerned: it was near, but that was about all.[12]

(1) *Theories of New Testament Eschatology*

The Incarnation brought about the great Christian differentia, *viz.* the Age to Come has now intercepted This Age in and through the Incarnation. From its very start, therefore,

---

[11] See Enoch 71:15, 2 Baruch 14:13; 2 Esdras 4:27, 7:12 f., 8:1; cp. Mt. 12:32; Mk. 10:30, etc.

[12] See, among others, R. H. Charles, *Eschatology: Hebrew, Jewish and Christian*, London, Black, 1899.

Christian Eschatology becomes a Christological phenomenon, and cannot be understood apart from the Christ. In the life, ministry, death and resurrection of Jesus, the future becomes interwoven with the present. The Incarnation precipitates "the final event"—the determinative event which not only reveals the meaning of the whole[13] but consummates the whole. The eschatological wheel is set in motion.

This is the general understanding of the New Testament. However, various views have been expressed on Christian Eschatology by various scholars in an attempt to provide solutions to two of the most difficult elements in Jesus' view of the future—its apocalyptic character, and its imminence. The solution of Consistent Eschatology, as favoured by Schweitzer,[14] involves the following elements: apocalyptic is an essential part of the message of the Kingdom as proclaimed by Jesus; this message is exclusively eschatological—the Kingdom is not in any sense a present reality; and Jesus thought that the inbreaking of the Kingdom was imminent.

Ernest von Dobschütz reacted against Schweitzer and put forward a non-eschatological interpretation of the Kingdom, advocating what he called "a transmuted Eschatology",[15] viz. that what Jewish Eschatology promised is "already at hand in the lifetime of Jesus . . . what was expected as an external change is taken inwardly". "In Jesus was fulfilled whatever was expected for the messianic time." This prepared the way for Dodd, who went further and propounded his doctine of a "realized eschatology".[16] In dealing with the parables of Jesus, and the apostolic preaching, Dodd goes to the extreme of over-emphasizing the "realization" of the Kingdom of God;[17] nevertheless, his interpretation of the parables and the apostolic Kerygma has made a great contribution to New Testament

---

[13] Cp. C. K. Barrett, "New Testament Eschatology", in *Scottish Journal of Theology*, Vol. VI, No. 2, June, 1953, p. 136.

[14] A. Schweitzer, *The Mystery of the Kingdom*, London, Black, 1925; and *The Quest of the Historical Jesus*, London, Black, 1910.

[15] E. von Dobschütz, *The Eschatology of the Gospels*, London, Hodder & Stoughton, 1910.

[16] C. H. Dodd "The This-Worldly Kingdom of God in our Lord's Teaching", in *Theology*, Vol. XIV, No. 83, 1927, pp. 258–260; *The Parables of the Kingdom*, London, Nisbet, 1935; *The Apostolic Preaching and its Developments*, London, Hodder & Stoughton, 1936; and *The Mind of Paul*, Manchester U.P., 1936.

[17] Dodd modified his position, in *The Coming of Christ*, Cambridge U.P., 1951.

scholarship. Attempts have been made,[18] though not always satisfactorily, to strike a balance between Schweitzer's and Dodd's positions.[19]

Glasson argues strongly that the doctrine of the Parousia is foreign to the Old Testament, the Apocrypha and the teaching of Jesus.[20] Robinson comes to the same conclusion, but from a different argument, pointing out that Jesus did not teach another coming, nor is it found in the earliest preaching and creeds of the Church.[21] Robinson advocates "inaugurated Eschatology", with the eventual reduction of all things to Christ. Bultmann's "reinterpreted Eschatology" tries to interpret history from the point of view of Eschatology, whereby the latter swallows up the former.[22]

In *Christ and Time*,[23] Cullmann interprets Eschatology in terms of a *Heilsgeschichte* built around the notion that Christ is the mid-point in a linear conception of Time. Accordingly, the "D-Day" is over, and only the final victory is to come. He draws a sharp distinction between *ho kairos* and *ho chronos*. While this approach certainly adds much to our understanding of Christian Eschatology, one cannot support it wholeheartedly since it is based on a partially false premise. There is not a single but multiple concept of Time in the Bible, and the distinction between the two Greek words for Time is not always so sharply drawn in the New Testament.[24]

There is no single or consistent view of Time in the Bible, nor does the Bible concern itself with what Time is. Several views exist, and only a few examples will suffice for our purposes. In the Lucan writings, there is a clear chronological account of the life, ministry, death, resurrection and departure of our Lord, followed by the Church in Jerusalem expanding towards the

---

[18] E.g., C. J. Cadoux, *The Historic Mission of Jesus*, London, Lutterworth Press, 1941; H. A. Guy, *The New Testament Doctrine of the 'Last Things'*, London, O.U.P. 1948; and R. H. Fuller, *The Mission and Achievement of Jesus*, London S.C.M. Press, 1954.

[19] For further discussion, see N. Perrin, *The Kingdom of God in the Teaching of Jesus*, London, S.C.M. Press, 1963.

[20] T. F. Glasson, *The Second Advent*, London, Epworth Press, 1945.

[21] J. A. T. Robinson, *Jesus and His Coming*, London, S.C.M. Press, 1957.

[22] R. Bultmann, *History and Eschatology*, London, Nelson, 1957.

[23] Engl. trans., 1951.

[24] For further discussion, see J. Barr, *Biblical Words for Time*, London, S.C.M. Press, 1962. Cullmann's views also are criticized by R. Bultmann, in *Theologische Literaturzeitung*, Vol. 73, 1948, under the title "Heilsgeschichte and Geschichte".

uttermost parts of the earth. This could be spoken of as a linear conception of Time:[25] but in Ecclesiastes we find a cyclic view of Time:[26] "what has been is what will be . . . and there is nothing new under the sun", and "that which is, already has been." In the Fourth Gospel we are being constantly confronted by Eternity in whose presence Time seems to shrink.

(2) The Eschatology of the Gospels

The Incarnation means, *inter alia*, that The Age to Come has intruded into This Age. The two overlap at present, but This Age is eschatologically being replaced entirely by the Age to Come. Probably the final changeover is realised at the point of the Parousia. One might illustrate this point diagrammatically:

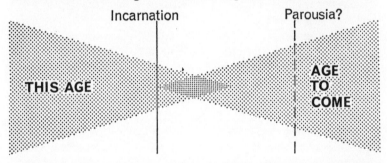

Incarnation   Parousia?

THIS AGE   AGE TO COME

This great happening cannot be explained away by a single linear conception of Time. New Testament Eschatology has both historical and ultra-historical dimensions, with the Cross at its heart. It is to this that the life and ministry of our Lord point: "So must the Son of Man be lifted up."[27] The Cross is the birth-pangs of the eschatological community: "And I, when I am lifted up from the earth, will draw all men to myself."[28] Upon the cross is fulfilled all that is needed to usher in the New Age, and from there Jesus makes one of His last utterances: "It is finished."[29]

In His own Person and ministry, Jesus actually brings in the Age to Come.[30] His works of healing, raising the dead,

[25] Cp. J. Manek, "The Biblical Concept of Time and our Gospels", in *New Testament Studies*, Vol. VI, No. 1, October, 1959.
[26] 1:4–11, 3:1–8, 15, etc.   [27] Jn. 3: 14 f.
[28] Jn. 12: 32.   [29] Jn. 19: 30.
[30] Mt. 11: 12–14; Lk. 7: 22 f, 16.16, etc.

opening the eyes of the blind, preaching the Gospel, etc., are concrete signs of the New Age: they are eschatological activities. His Baptism at the hands of John the Baptizer is an act of fulfilment;[31] His ministry is one of fulfilment which also precipitates the arrival of the Kingdom of God.[32] The Gospel of Jesus is fulfilment.[33] In His preaching and teaching, Jesus uses vocabulary which is heavily loaded with eschatological meaning, such as the Kingdom of God, repent, judgement, etc. He brings the Kingdom of God into human history, and what He is and is doing are clear signs of its arrival: ". . . the Kingdom of God has come upon you."[34] Another dimension is that, paradoxically, the Kingdom "is not coming with signs to be observed",[35] nor can it be pinpointed to either spatial[36] or temporal dimensions.[37] The Passion is the final epitome of the end of the old era and the birth of the new.[38]

While the Gospels are clear on the fact that the eschatological days are here, there is a major paradox which runs through the entire New Testament. The Kingdom of God has come,[39] but that is only the beginning which guarantees and points to the future consummation.[40] So paradoxically, the End has come and the End is yet to be. Jesus stretches human history like a line between two posts: the Cross and the Parousia. As He is the Bringer, so He will be the Consummator of the Age to Come. The Eucharist, which forms the central moment in Christian worship, is celebrated as unveiling the whole eschatological drama from the Cross to the Consummation of the ages: "For as often as you eat this bread and drink the cup, you proclaim the Lord's death until He comes."[41] The Cross plunges Christians into an eschatological tension of fulfilment and promises or expectations. Christians are, in the words of St. Paul, the ones "upon whom the end of the ages has come"[42] since the eschatological Adam[43] has appeared at the fullness of Time.[44]

Jesus brings the Kingdom of God into human history, and

---

[31] Mt. 3: 15. [32] Mk. 1: 15. [33] Mk. 1: 14 f., Lk. 4: 16–21.
[34] Lk. 11: 20. [35] Lk. 17: 20. [36] Lk. 17: 21.
[37] Lk. 19: 11–27, Mt. 25: 14–30, Acts 1: 6 f. [38] Lk. 12: 50.
[39] Mt. 12: 28. [40] Cp. Mt. 24: 14.
[41] 1 Cor. 11: 26 (this verse comes from the earliest tradition concerning the Eucharist).
[42] 1 Cor. 10: 11. [43] 1 Cor. 15: 45. [44] Gal. 4: 4.

it is in this light that Dodd interprets the parables. But precisely because it is an eschatological phenomenon, the Kingdom is both present and future and Time does not exhaust it: it is an eternal reality. Men must enter the Kingdom now. It is in the Fourth Gospel, more than in the Synoptics, that the full and practical implications of Eschatology emerge. Here, there is a balance between realized and futurist Eschatologies. The Day of Judgment is partly realized,[45] and is partly to come;[46] the Resurrection is a reality both now[47] and on "the last Day";[48] the Holy Spirit (Paraclete) is given Now,[49] and yet He will come when the Father and the Son send Him.[50] When it is realized Eschatology, as Moule has pointed out, it tends to be chiefly on an individual rather than collective level.[51] Thus Life Eternal becomes a reality when it is apprehended personally by the individual, even though it is shed for the whole cosmos; individuals encounter Jesus and are changed.[52] The passing from death to life as a *fait accompli* is in terms of individuals,[53] as is also judgement or acquittal[54] and resurrection.[55] But there is also the future dimension, which is portrayed in terms of the collective in the Fourth Gospel. The life, ministry and the Parousia of Jesus form a unity, so that His ministry is an act of sacrifice, the Cross in His exaltation in glory, the coming or giving of the Spirit is indeed the Parousia of Christ,[56] though a future consummation is not precluded.[57]

(3) *The Eschatology of the Acts, Epistles and Revelation*

The Acts of the Apostles shows closely the conviction of the early Church that the Age to Come has dawned in the life and ministry of Jesus.[58] The Age of Fulfilment has come

[45] Jn. 3: 18 f., 5: 24. [46] 5: 28 f.; 8:51; 12:48; 11: 24–26.
[47] 5: 25; 11: 25. [48] 5: 28 f.; 6: 39, 44, etc. [49] 20: 22.
[50] 14: 16, 26; 15: 26; 16: 13 f., etc.
[51] For further discussion see C. F. D. Moule, "The Individualism of the Fourth Gospel", in *Novum Testamentum*, Vol. V, Fasc. 3/3, 1962, pp. 171–190.
[52] The two disciples, 1:38; Peter, 1: 42; Philip, 1: 43; Nathanael, 1: 47; Nicodemus, 3: 1–15; the Samaritan woman, chap. 4; the cripple by the pool of Bethesda, chap. 5; the woman caught in adultery, 8: 3–11; etc.
[53] 5: 24, etc. [54] 3: 18; 5: 24. [55] Ch. 11.
[56] Jn. 14: 18 f., 21–23, etc. [57] Cp. 14: 3.
[58] See further, C. H. Dodd, *The Apostolic Preaching and Its Developments*, 1936; and H. J. Cadbury, "Acts and Eschatology", contributed to the Dodd Festschrift, edited by W. D. Davies and D. Daube: *The Background of the New Testament and its Eschatology*, London, O.U.P., 1956. This work will be cited here as the Dodd *Festschrift*.

through Jesus Christ.[59] The Holy Spirit is the sure sign of this realization.[60] However, the Consummation is "not yet".[61] Between the Cross and the Parousia, the Church must expand from Jerusalem "to the end of the earth". The missionary impulse is intimately linked with eschatological expectations.[62]

Paul's Thessalonian epistles, mainly due to circumstances, deal with a futurist and apocalyptic Eschatology, and Paul himself expects to be alive at the moment of the Parousia which is imminent.[63] In his other epistles, the Parousia retires into the background, but it is never dismissed. Of more immediate importance are the human institutions like the family, slavery, the state, disputes, the Church and the life of the eschatological community. In Ephesians and Colossians, the community is here to stay, and the Parousia coincides with the reconciliation of all things in Christ.[64] Jesus is the Firstborn[65] in the New Age, the nucleus of the new creation around whom the Church, His Body, grows.[66] Christians are the product of an eschatological event, the special people "upon whom the end of the ages has come".[67] The Holy Spirit is the eschatological *arrabon*[68] linking the Jesus of Nazareth with His community the Church. What has happened to Jesus has, *ipso facto*, happened to all those who are incorporated into Him. The Christians are crucified with Christ,[69] raised with Him,[70] glorified with Him[71] and are to come with Him at His Parousia.[72] The benefits of the Age to Come can and must be assimilated now by the one who is in Christ. This appropriation, however, is always in hope and expectation. The Church, existing between the Cross and the Parousia, celebrates the Sacraments of Baptism and the Eucharist, both of which are intensely eschatological.[73] The Consummation, the final goal

---

[59] 2: 14–39; 3: 13–26, etc.   [60] 2: 33; 5: 32.
[61] 3: 21; 10: 42.   [62] 1: 6–8; cp. Mt. 28: 19 f., 24: 14.
[63] 1 Thess. 1: 10; 2: 19; 3: 13; 4: 13–18; 5: 23; 2 Thess. 1: 7–10; 2: 1–4.
[64] Col. 1: 20; cp. Eph. 1: 9 f.   [65] Col. 1: 15.   [66] Eph. 4: 16.
[67] 1 Cor. 10: 11.   [68] Gk. an earnest, 2 Cor. 1: 22; 5: 5; Eph. 1: 13.
[69] Gal. 2: 20.   [70] Col. 2: 12.   [71] Rom. 8: 30.   [72] 1 Thess. 3: 13; 4: 17.
[73] A great deal has been written on the Eschatology of the Sacraments. Among others see N. Clark, *An Approach to the Theology of the Sacraments*, London, S.C.M. Press, 1956; C. F. D. Moule, "The Judgment Theme in the Sacraments", in the Dodd *Festschrift*, 1956; and *Worship in the New Testament*, London, Lutterworth Press, 1961.

to which all must lead,[74] never disappears from Paul's thinking, however intense these other experiences become. Paul's eschatology is essentially the same as the eschatology of the Gospels.

In Hebrews there is a sharp tension between Fulfilment and the "not yet". The Incarnation has precipitated the eschatological (last) days,[75] and the Parousia will consummate this process.[76] A new and better Covenant now replaces the Old Covenant,[77] bringing with it a new and better hope.[78] The Cross, a once-for-all event, marks the end of the evil Age and the beginning of the Age to Come.[79] Christians already taste, here and now, "the goodness of the word of God and the powers of the age to come",[80] and are already experiencing the eschatological sabbath rest.[81] Between the Cross and the Parousia, the Christians are pilgrims and so journey, walking by faith[82] as the last days draw near.[83] But their experience is so real that they have actually "come to Mount Zion and to the city of the living God, the heavenly Jerusalem, and to innumerable angels in festal gathering, and to the assembly of the first-born who are enrolled in heaven . . . and to Jesus, the mediator of a new covenant".[84]

The eschatology of the epistle of St. James is mainly futuristic. Accordingly, the last days are still in the future, and the dominant event is not primarily what took place on the Cross but "the coming of the Lord" which is imminent and for which Christians must wait patiently.[85] The Incarnation did, however, bring in the new day when God "of his own will brought us forth by the word of truth that we should be a kind of first fruits of his creatures".[86] Christians are to practise true religion of love and obedience, for faith without works is dead.[87]

The author of 1 Peter is conscious that divine intervention in human history has occurred in Jesus Christ,[88] epitomized in the eschatological community which has been brought

---

[74] Col. 3: 4; Phil. 3: 20 f.; 1 Cor. 15: 28; Eph. 1: 12 f.
[75] 1: 2. [76] 9: 28. [77] 7: 22; 8: 6 f., 10: 9 f.
[78] 7: 19. [79] 9: 26; 10: 9. [80] 6: 5. [81] 4: 9 f.
[82] 6: 18 f.; 10: 19, 22. [83] 10: 25.
[84] 12: 21–24. See further discussion by C. K. Barrett, "The Eschatology of the Epistle to the Hebrews", in the Dodd *Festschrift*, 1956.
[85] 5: 3 ff. [86] 1: 18. [87] 1: 22; 2: 8 ff.
[88] 1: 3 ff.

forth.[89] We live in the eschatological time[90] into which the prophets enquired.[91] As a result of the Incarnation we experience, here and now, both salvation and judgement.[92] Through Baptism, believers have tasted their destiny;[93] but there is yet to come the full measure of grace at the revelation of Jesus Christ.[94] Christians are aliens and exiles[95] living under the compulsion of a great urgency because "the end of all things is at hand".[96] The Last Day simply consummates what is being appropriated now.[97]

In 2 Peter the author is positive that believers are granted to partake of the divine nature,[98] though their entry into the Kingdom is still in the future.[99] The day of the Lord will be accompanied by a physical upheaval in which the universe will be incinerated, but behind this unsparing destruction lie "new heavens and a new earth",[100] ready to replace the old. Mockers are impatient that the expected Parousia has not yet arrived, and in defence the author introduces a chronological element to combat such misrepresentation, to the effect that "with the Lord one day is a thousand years" and *vice versa*, and that God is in fact waiting for all to repent.[101]

In the first Johannine epistle, Jesus Christ is central, and His message is urgent because this is "the last [eschatological] hour".[102] The old order is passing away,[103] and the believer in Christ is already the child of God. All that remains for the believer is that "it does not yet appear what we shall be, but we know when he appears we shall be like him, for we shall see him as he is".[104] The End only winds up what already is the experience of those who abide in Christ.

The Eschatology of the book of Revelation is almost exclusively futuristic and apocalyptic. The accomplished work of Christ is allowed only a minor place. Through His blood, Christians are "made . . . a kingdom, priests to his God and Father",[105] and share "in Jesus the tribulation and the kingdom and the patient endurance".[106] The overcoming churches

---

[89] 2: 9 f.   [90] 1: 20.   [91] 1: 10–12.   [92] 1: 5 f.
[93] 5: 10.   [94] 1: 13; 5: 4.   [95] 2: 11.   [96] 4: 7.
[97] See for further discussion, E. G. Selwyn, "Eschatology in 1 Peter", in the Dodd *Festschrift*, 1956.
[98] 1: 4.   [99] 1: 11.   [100] 3: 10–13.   [101] 3: 3 ff.
[102] 2: 18.   [103] 2: 17.   [104] 3: 1 f.   [105] 1: 6.
[106] 1: 9.

receive their reward in the future;[107] the Jerusalem above is yet to descend,[108] and the ransomed are to reign in the future.[109] The saints under the altar cry out, "How long?"[110] as they wait for the *eschaton* to arrive. But the book has a cosmic scope for the Gospel: all nations ascribe praise to Jesus;[111] all creatures recognize Him,[112] and the Gospel is proclaimed to all.[113] In the End, all things are made new,[114] and Jesus appears as the Mighty Conqueror, the Lamb of the New Jerusalem.[115]

(4) *Conclusions and Consequences of New Testament Eschatology*

a. The New Testament Eschatology is based and centred upon the fact of fulfilment through the Incarnation of Jesus Christ. This runs right through the New Testament.

b. The New Testament does not, however, lose sight of the Final Consummation of what has already begun to take place. Different pictures and metaphors are used to refer to it; the term "the Second Coming" is not one of them.[116]

c. The Church exists between the two poles: the Cross and the Parousia. Meanwhile, she has to appropriate the benefits of the Age to Come through, among other things, the Sacraments of Baptism and the Eucharist both of which are intensely eschatological. Eternal life, Resurrection, Glory, Faith, etc., which are being realized here and now, point towards the final goal when all things will ripen to their Consummation. Here we have only a foretaste, the first fruits and the guarantee of the whole. The Holy Spirit is the guarantee *par excellence*, given to the eschatological community.[117] The Church's missionary outreach is an integral eschatological compulsion.

d. For the Christian, death is made impotent, for he is raised with Christ in Baptism.[118] He belongs to the new humanity in Christ,[119] which is part of the cosmic New Creation.[120] This Age, with all its implications, is giving way to the Age to Come with all its eternal realities, and the process will come to a climax at the point of the Parousia.

---

[107] 2: 7, 11, 23, 27, etc.   [108] 3: 12; 21: 2.   [109] 5: 9 f.
[110] 6: 10.   [111] 6: 9; 7: 9 f.   [112] 5: 13.
[113] 14: 6.   [114] 21: 1, 3.   [115] 21: 22–22: 5.
[116] This term appears first in the writings of Justin Martyr in the second century.
[117] Jn. 14: 26; 15: 26; Acts 2: 16 ff.; 2 Cor. 1: 22; 5: 5; Eph. 1: 13 f.
[118] Rom. 6: 3–11, cp. Gal. 2: 19 f.
[119] 2 Cor. 5: 17.   [120] Rev. 21: 1; 2 Peter 3: 13.

e. Eschatology is ultimately a christological phenomenon. Where terms like Heaven, Glory, Eternal Life, Resurrection, Judgement, etc., are used, they must be understood both eschatologically and christologically. The New Testament Hereafter makes sense only in a christological context, since death is conquered by Christ who becomes "a life-giving spirit";[121] the Resurrection is not only effected through Jesus but inheres in Him;[122] Heaven is heavenly in so far as it is the city of God and of Christ, and it is dominated by God and the Lamb:[123] the final crown of Glory is meaningful only in so far as it is Christ's Glory being shared among those who are "in Christ". The after life is not some experience kept in store for the Christian to inherit only after he has died; rather, through the Incarnation it has intruded into the here-and-now. To be incorporated into Christ, through Faith and Baptism, is, *inter alia*, to be transferred to Christ's Kingdom,[124] and to share in all the consequences of this shattering experience.

III. ATTEMPT TO LINK UP AFRICAN AND CHRISTIAN ESCHATOLOGIES

This is undoubtedly the most difficult part of this paper, and at the same time perhaps the most crucial. One can do no more than point the way, as it touches, like so many other topics, the very heart of the Christian presence in Africa. My comments are based on the assumption that many items in African traditional life, ideas and practices can and have to be taken as a *praeparatio evangelica*.[125] Certain aspects of African Eschatology may profitably be linked up with Christian Eschatology.

1. "The End" is lacking in African Eschatology. But in Christian Eschatology we find it centred, as it is, in Jesus Christ; to this the New Testament bears a clear witness. Life is not simply a natural rhythm of the cycle of days, months, and years or of birth, initiation, death, etc.; the New Testament is quite clear on this issue. According to its teaching, there is a Beginning and there will be an End, and the Incarnation intro-

---

[121] 1 Cor. 15: 45.   [122] Jn. 11: 25; cp. Rev. 1 18.
[123] Rev. 21: 22 f.; 22: 1–5.   [124] Col. 1: 13.
[125] Some writers would object to the idea of aspects of traditional life being a *praeparatio evangelica*, foremost of whom is H. Kraemer, e.g. in *The Christian Message in a non-Christian World*, London, Edinburgh House Press, 1938.

duces into this present life the impact and the reality of the End-things. Thus, we are the one "upon whom the end of the ages has come",[126] and in Revelation Jesus is categorically spoken of as "the first and the last".[127] But Jesus is not simply a natural, mechanical termination; rather, He is the One in whom all things find their meaningful End, "the Beginning and the End". He is the teleological meaning of all being. Hence, all things are to be summed up in Him.[128] This process is hard at work now; the Incarnation has released into human history all the benefits of the Age to Come, so that a new Creation is emerging and only the Consummation is awaited.

This fact introduces into African thinking both eternal realities and a future dimension of Time. It is not a future so much in terms of a distant goal simply to be hoped for and coveted, but a future dimension which is both present and future because its realities are eternal and cannot be exhausted in this life. In Christ the life of man becomes not simply a mechanical or natural succession of events in an unending rhythm. The New Testament shows us that man is a growing creature whose full stature is in Christ; and in this experience, the question of a rhythmic cycle of nature is outmoded. The *eschaton* must invade the African world, not to destroy or colonize but to fulfil, to inject into its cosmology Christian realities. Africa has an Eschatology, but it has no teleology, and this is an area where Christian Eschatology can make a radical contribution to God's natural revelation in Africa. Eschatology without teleology is as empty as a house without furniture.

2. African languages seem to lack a future dimension of Time, beyond a short distance. Although Western education and modern national development plans are creating this new dimension in African thinking and life, we are still faced with a major question of how to introduce meaningfully those eternal and eschatological realities which we find in the New Testament. Without going into a full discussion of the matter, it would seem that the Sacraments of Baptism and the Eucharist present themselves clearly as the areas where both temporal and eternal realities meet, and the media through which the temporal may catch glimpses of the eternal. The outward signs are performed and the elements handled in terms of the

[126] 1 Cor. 10: 11.   [127] Rev. 22: 13.   [128] Eph. 1: 9 f.

concrete and historical: water, bread, wine—elements that can be perceived through all the five senses of Man. Through their sacramental use, these elements epitomize eternal realities. They are the nutshell of the Gospel, and dramatize before us the entire phenomenon of the Church from the Cross to the Parousia.

Many African peoples penetrate into the spirit-world through offerings, libation and sacrifices, thus using the material as the bridge with the spiritual. Have we not then, in Christian theology and practice, an even more noble set of material elements which, within the sacramental context, speak to us of, and dramatize before us, the realities which are not only spiritual but eternal, infinitely and intimately bound up with the Person and life of Jesus Christ? The Sacraments are christological and eschatological, and they, more than any other aspects of the Christian life, convey to us the eternal realities revealed in the Incarnation. The Church in Africa must certainly discover the theology of the Sacraments, and apply it in the work of evangelization, for the ground is already prepared.

3. The Hereafter in African thought is a natural form of immortality, with its life being a carbon copy of the present. But, as we have already observed, this is not so with Christianity, whose Hereafter is a life of the Resurrection. This Resurrection is not a natural, mechanical and inevitable form of life but in reality it is life resurrected to Life, real Life at its very source, the Life whose nature and essential character are none other than "everlasting", "eternal".[129] This is something entirely new to African thought, since there is neither the World to Come nor *eternal* as opposed to *temporal* realities. To introduce eternal realities into African thought is to introduce something not only new but revolutionary. Already this is being done, but not in the most suitable, or even biblical form. One often finds a cheap form of evangelization which simply *sells* the Gospel by promising believers a Utopia in heaven where an essentially carnal life of pleasure and leisure replaces this present life of sorrow and pain. This approach promises heavenly mansions

---

[129] The Greek word *aionios*, translated "eternal", certainly includes the idea of "everlasting", but that is not where the emphasis lies. Its emphasis is on the eternal quality and quantity, belonging to the essence and nature of the World to Come, being grounded in the very nature of God Himself.

and all the other items which individuals may lack but wish to have in this life, and encourages a form of escapism. It is a cheapening of the Gospel, and it turns Jesus Christ into a Purveyor of souls from this to the next world. Sound evangelization must be rooted in a comprehensive and biblical Christology.

4. African sensitivity to the spirit-world is something that could enrich the rather impoverished type of Christianity which has come to us through Western thought and practice, in which the spirit-world is either dismissed altogether or put in the extreme background—except for spiritist cults which function outside the Church. The New Testament is extremely aware of the spirit-world and its nearness to the human world. Again and again Jesus encounters the spirits, and one of the eschatological signs of His presence and ministry is the exorcising of the spirits. The Cross is a cosmic struggle which involves not only the human rulers but the spiritual rulers and principalities. Our Christian warfare is not "against flesh and blood, but against the principalities, against the powers, against the world rulers of this present darkness, against the spiritual hosts of wickedness in the heavenly places."[130] Africa knows only too well that spirits exist and form an essential part of man's spiritual environment. The Gospel in Africa must address itself to the spirit-world as well and not to the human world alone.

Again, the Western Church, whose thought and traditions we have largely inherited, appears to be losing the ancient practice of remembering and praying for the dead in public worship (Diptychs), and has neglected the doctrine of "the Communion of Saints". Here, African traditional thought and practices may easily bring a renewal into the Church's life, with regard to the relationship between the departed and living Christians. In this area we need to rediscover the meaning and implications of Christ's cosmic victory on the Cross. Redemption is not simply for those who are alive in this world: its full implications must reach into the very roots of our peoples and nations, to redeem the *whole man*, which includes both the living, the living-dead and the spirits. Soteriological theology in Africa must bring under its umbrella the whole of African ontology which includes not only the human, but also the ani-

[130] Eph. 6: 12.

183

mal, plant and inanimate creation. According to African ontology, many of the so-called inanimate objects (like rocks, caves, ponds, stars, etc.) are teeming with life, animated by the spiritual beings. So man, with all his environment, must be included in the outreach of the Gospel message in Africa.

5. In traditional life there are many myths about the *Zamani* period—about death, the separation between heaven and earth, the severing of the links between God and man. As we pointed out, there are no corresponding myths of the *Endzeit*, by which what went wrong may be repaired. There is no *Endzeit*, and therefore there could not be myths about it. This is not a loss in natural revelation; it is simply an empty area of African thought which should readily be filled up with the Christian concepts of the *Endzeit*. In Christ death is vanquished; the separation between God and man is for ever bridged in His Incarnation.

This, then, is the completion of the story in which mythological knowledge tells us of the tragedies of the *Urzeit*, but leaves us without a solution to those tragedies. In traditional African life we have no choice but to accept death with all its sorrows; we have no choice but to accept the apparent alienation between God and man. Our forefathers found no myths for the *Endzeit*, however much they might have wished to find them. The New Testament supplies this missing link, not for the sake of mythology, but because the Incarnation makes it inevitable. We have to transmit this message: Africa's broken rope between Heaven and Earth is once and for all re-established in Christ; Africa's God who evidently withdrew from men to the heavens, has now come "down" to man, not only as the Son of God but also as Immanuel, God with us; and Death which came so early into man's existence, and from which there was no escape, is now for ever abolished. Beyond it lies not the dusty ruins of the conflict, but the shining light of the Resurrection, to which creation and mankind are invited and destined in Christ.

CONTRIBUTORS

THE REV. E. A. ADEOLU ADEGBOLA	*Principal of Immanuel College, Ibadan, Nigeria.*
MR. SAMUEL A. AMISSAH, O.B.E.	*General Secretary of the All Africa Conference of Churches.*
THE REV. KWESI A. DICKSON	*Lecturer in the Department for the Study of Religions, University of Ghana.*
THE REV. PAUL ELLINGWORTH	*Formerly lecturer in the Faculté de Théologie Protestante, Yaoundé, Cameroun.*
THE VERY REV. MGR. S. N. EZEANYA	*Formerly lecturer in the Crowther Department of Religion, University of Nigeria, Nsukka.*
THE REV. PROF. E. BOLAJI IDOWU	*Head of the Department of Religious Studies, University of Ibadan, Nigeria.*
THE REV. R. BUANA KIBONGI	*Principal of the Ecole de Théologie de Ngouedi-Loutété, Congo-Brazzaville.*
THE REV. PROF. JOHN S. MBITI	*Head of the Department of Religion, Makerere University College, Uganda.*
THE REV. DR. VINCENT MULAGO	*Lecturer in the Faculté de Théologie, and Director of the Centre d'Etudes des Religions Africaines, Université Lovanium, Congo-Kinshasa.*
THE REV. CANON HARRY SAWYERR, C.B.E.	*Principal of Fourah Bay College, University of Sierra Leone.*
THE REV. SWAILEM SIDHOM	*Director of the Limuru Conference Centre, Kenya.*

INDEX